SOUTHERN CALIFORNIA
a guide for the eyes™

Southern California:
A Guide for the Eyes

First Edition
©2015 Elisa Parhad
Photographs by Elisa Parhad unless otherwise noted. Some photographs are used by permission. These works are the property of the original copyright owners.

Cover photograph by Susanne Duffner.

Printed in China

ISBN: 978-0-9820497-2-3
Library of Congress Control Number: 2014952346

Published by EyeMuse Books
1480 North Mentor Avenue
Pasadena, CA 91104
www.eyemusebooks.com

11111530

Southern California

a guide for the eyes™

Enjoy, Donna!

Elisa Parhad

2021

eyemuse books

Pasadena, California

TO MARSAIS, MY CONSTANT COMPANION

TABLE OF CONTENTS

PREFACE

When I created the *Guide for the Eyes* series in 2008, I hadn't considered that it could forever change the way I experience a new place. The inspiration for an at-a-glance cultural guide came to me after I lived in Japan, where I needed help decoding the cultural and natural landscape. The concept evolved into a visual and textual presentation of 100 items frequently found within a region, including foods, crafts, architectural details, and nature. This simple formula would become a new way of thinking for me. Every trip turned into an excuse for lessons in history and geography and a hunt for authentic expressions of regional identity, whether I found myself in Venice Beach or Venice, Italy.

The timing of this transformation coincided with a move to Los Angeles. A list of 100 items crucial to the character of Southern California began to assemble in my head soon after I arrived. I couldn't have stopped myself if I had tried—the area is a wonderland for an exploring daytripper. Fusion foods, themed environments, monuments of modernism, movie history, and breathtaking mountain and canyon vistas await around every corner. I marveled at this strange and new environment.

The research and photography for this project permeated my daily life, creating adventures out of the most ordinary outings. If I went to a movie, I'd try to go to one of Los Angeles's historic **movie palaces**. If I needed to hit an outlet mall, I'd go to the one in a 1930s-era tire factory fashioned into an Assyrian citadel and bring my camera along. Even the act of eating out came with an agenda. When a pregnancy-induced craving for matzo ball soup hit, I went out of my way to make it to Langer's Delicatessen— a mecca for **pastrami** lovers in downtown Los Angeles. This wasn't pregnancy logic—I was multitasking my way around a specific hunger *and* my curiosity about a food that is an unexpected fixture in SoCal. The slow-cooked meat is a common offering at non-franchised fast-food joints, a key ingredient in the Oki dog (Los Angeles's own peculiar gut bomb), and a favorite sandwich insert within greater Los Angeles's thriving Jewish deli scene. Thankfully, I did not ingest the famous #19 pastrami sandwich on that visit—I had labor pains after savoring my soup and was soon off to the hospital to welcome my son.

Being a new mother, I suddenly had another territory to navigate— Babyland. At this point in the project I had only a skeleton table of contents and loads of notes. The finished project required 100 short write-ups about a range of topics, and 100 photographs to illustrate them. This meant that I had a 200-item-long to-do list that could only be addressed between diaper changes, feedings, burpings, and storytime. Writing was scheduled during naps, after bedtime, and anytime I could squeeze it in, but photography was exclusively together time for my son and me. For whatever I had to capture with a camera, we'd head off to find it. Across the counties of Ventura, Riverside, Los Angeles, Orange, San Bernardino, and San Diego, we went to **beaches**, monuments, iconic buildings, orange groves, museums, gardens, restaurants, **theme parks**, **swimming pools**, and **strip malls**. From Anza-Borrego National Park to Zuma Beach, we took more than 2,500 photographs together, about 75 percent of which were framed with my son's head in a carrier just below the lens.

In addition to the difficulties of getting anything done with a baby in tow, the diversity of Southern California made the work feel daunting. The writing and photography has at times felt like some eccentric collection of disjointed bits and bobs. The region is a big place that holds whole worlds within it. How could I possibly capture it all? This question concerned me until I realized that to capture it all isn't the point. The *Guide for the Eyes* books are meant to provide the beginning clues to what makes a place tick. I made sure to mention specific people, attractions, and phenomena within each topic so that readers can further explore the often inspiring, unbelievable, and fantastical stories behind them. I am forever grateful for these enriching and memorable tales as well as for the opportunity to publish about my new(ish) home, Southern California. My hope is that this book

My son—one year old at the time—takes a break from his carrier at Vasquez Rocks Natural Area Park near Agua Dulce, CA

brings answers to questions that readers never knew they had, as it has for me.

INTRODUCTION

Southern California needs almost no introduction. This fabled land is renowned for its laid-back vibe, lifestyles of the rich and famous, rampant car culture, enviable climate, and apocalyptic natural disasters. The **palm trees**, backyard **swimming pools**, and **surf** breaks are broadcast globally, forming the window through which the world views the region. This familiarity is increasing as the rest of the planet becomes more and more car dependent, making Los Angeles's defining look—a hodgepodge of **billboards**, **freeways**, and **strip malls**—stock imagery in major cities worldwide. Both the exports of the motion picture industry and global suburbanization have given the region the look of everywhere and nowhere all at once.

This near-mythic El Dorado at the edge of the continent spans from Santa Barbara in the north to the Mexican border in the south, from the desert to the sea, encompassing a staggering diversity of landscapes, peoples, and traditions. The multiplicity of terrain—from the megalopolis of Greater Los Angeles to vast expanses of barren scrubland—is mirrored by a multiplicity of cultures and peoples. Even before the arrival of the Spanish in 1769, 500 or so Native American groups counted more than 100 languages among them. Following the Spanish, there has been a continuous stream of newcomers seeking fame, riches, a new beginning, and the unique local culture of tolerance and innovation, adding to regional heterogeneity. Today the land is home to some of the world's largest communities of Mexicans, Iranians, Filipinos, Vietnamese, Armenians, Koreans, and Samoans outside their home countries (to name a few nationalities), making it one of the first states in the country (behind Hawaii) with a minority-majority.

Each group has left its mark—Japanese fishermen likely influenced the fish **taco**, Australian miners sparked a fascination for **eucalyptus**, and Indian philosophies have greatly added to the Southland's spiritual repertoire—but none has flavored the Southern California experience as much as Old Spain and Mexico. Hispanic contributions include the red-tiled and stucco buildings that mimic the Spanish **missions** and Mexican-style haciendas, the Latino signs and symbols that permeate West Coast **graffiti** style, and the **murals** by Mexican artists who inspired the local tradition of mural-making. Even as this heritage is reconfigured for new generations, icons such as the Day of the Dead, the **Virgin of Guadalupe**, **customized cars**, **food trucks**, and many, many Mexican staples—**tamales**, **tacos**, **burritos**, and **chips and salsa**—are constant reminders of our south-of-the-border ties.

What Hispanic influence is to SoCal culture, the car is to the SoCal environment. What is now covered with suburban sprawl had been a treeless scrubland framed by low mountains a little more than 200 years ago. In 1781 the new pueblo of Los Angeles had just 44 official residents; in 2015 the city had nearly four million. Through gold, **citrus**, and oil rushes, multiple real estate booms, and population surges, Southern California has been a veritable canvas for the whims of builders who created an eclectic quilt of structures in varying shapes and styles. With the rise of the automobile after World War II came explosive growth, and the convenience of the car became the dominant consideration in the building of roadways, buildings, and homes. The result is a landscape optimized for four-wheeled travel, complete with a slew of car-

inspired innovations—**freeways, strip malls**, drive-ins, drive-thrus, motels, programmatic structures (commercial follies designed to tease attention away from the road and onto a business), **California ranch homes**, **billboards**, and **dingbat apartment** buildings. Before the car began to shape the growth of Southern Californian cities, an extensive network of streetcars helped to create distinct neighborhoods built around trolley stops. Cars helped to fill in the undeveloped gaps, creating near-continuous suburban growth surrounding Los Angeles and San Diego. Rails no longer connect this wide sea of homes, businesses, **billboards**, and **palm trees**—concrete **freeways** do.

There are many reasons so many

people flocked to Southern California in a relatively short period of time, but one of the biggest attractions has always been the climate and the corresponding culture. Individuals clamored for warm winters where **citrus fruits** thrived and weekends could be spent by a Palm Springs motel **pool**. Businessmen chose to locate **aerospace** and motion picture industries in the region in part for the good weather, which was needed for flight tests and early filmmaking. Consistently pleasant temperatures not only allowed for outdoor living and leisure year round, they were vital for cultivating the values of openness and optimism that only added to Southern California's appeal for artists, entrepreneurs, eccentrics, or those who simply wanted a fresh start. New residents found that the inhibition and formality that characterized the Midwest and East Coast could be thrown off like an old winter coat. This freedom from established traditions, far from the opinions of friends and family, as well as the power structure of blue-blood high society, fueled trendsetting explorations and experiments in domesticity, architecture, spirituality, health, commerce, technology, fashion, and recreation. The area was made to be the perfect pop-culture incubator, and it remains so today.

The many successes that came from this open-mindedness gave the region a powerful national voice, and the motion picture industry provided the microphone to enhance it. Local fads and fashions showcased by movie stars both on- and off-screen were picked up nationwide. Whether it was the **margarita**, **surfing**, or patio entertaining, Hollywood and its stars helped to widen the audience for SoCal's new ideas for living. The skill sets that the industry brought to the economy—from wardrobe specialists to set designers—added to the realm of possibility in architecture and fashion, bringing glamour, extravagance, and whimsy to what could have been the domain of the mundane or the merely practical.

Even with its relatively short history, Southern California is awash in influences, all of which have shaped its landscape and charac-

ter. Within its vast space there are **bungalow** heavens, **modern** meccas, space travel manufacturers, quiet retreats, congested intersections, New Age meditation centers, crumbling **movie palaces**, **visionary environments**, the Entertainment Capitol of the World, the Happiest Place on Earth, and a surfers' paradise. SoCal has within it a little bit of everything, which can be anything for those of us who are here to embrace it.

ABOUT THIS BOOK

Before you begin, a few notes about the contents of this book:

- Each topic is listed categorically in the table of contents for easy reference and alphabetically on the pages to mimic their random discovery within the landscape.

- **Bold-face** words refer to another topic within the book.

- Many topics address folk traditions, which may vary greatly from region to region or even household to household. Generally, the most broadly accepted interpretations are described here.

- With the exception of a few food items, all photographs were taken on location as they were found (snapshot style) with minimal or no styling.

- EyeMuse Books worked with several photographers to provide a multi-perspective view of the region. We look forward to expanding this type of collaboration for future editions of this series.

There was something new and pervasive about the quality of the western light. The benign climate brought an almost romantic consciousness of nature. There was a sense of timelessness of being in a world apart—a world which could be remade in one's own vision—in which one's desired lifestyle could be realized and one's influence felt.

—Eudorah M. Moore
on California
in *California Design 1910*

An Ajax powder window display at a 99 Cents Only store in Los Angeles, CA • Alexander Vidal

99 CENT STORE

When entrepreneur David Gold (1932–2013) made the connection that consumers are more likely to buy something that is priced under a dollar rather than even a few cents more, an idea was born. In 1982 he opened the first "99 Cents Only" store near downtown Los Angeles. While the concept of stocking all products for a single price wasn't new, the approach was. Instead of offering one-off, oddball items, the retailer's large, brightly lit stores teem with name-brand, perishable goods and household items that have expired or been discontinued, allowing merchandise to be sold at a deep discount. Mr. Gold soon saw that the wealthy like to save money too. Many stores are easily accessible to this demographic, including the Beverly Hills adjacent location—the retailer's highest-grossing store. Due to rising costs and inflation, the company has had a single price increase, from 99.00 cents to 99.99 cents, in 2008.

As the largest and most successful single-price retailer in the country, 99 Cents Only stores are convenient, organized, and certainly affordable. Nonetheless, it's the imitator "98 Cent" and "99 Cents and Up" stores that are especially compelling. Funky, and tailored to their own neighborhood demographics, these stores offer shoppers all the delights of a treasure hunt—at 20 to 80 percent off. *See also Strip Mall.*

A Dragon capsule, manufactured at the SpaceX headquarters in Hawthorne, CA, is captured by the International Space Station above planet Earth • Courtesy of SpaceX and NASA

AEROSPACE ENGINEERING

Although the importance of aerospace engineering in Southern California is often overshadowed by the highly visible entertainment business, most historians would argue that no other industry has had a greater impact on the region's wealth, growth, economy, demographics, and culture. Northrop, Lockheed, Douglas, Hughes, SpaceX, and the Jet Propulsion Laboratory are just a handful of pioneering institutions that helped bring about legendary undertakings such as the F-1 rocket engine, the Apollo 11 spacecraft, the B-2 Spirit stealth bomber, and the space shuttle *Endeavour*, stretching the bounds of human possibility and imagination. The extraordinary innovation, risk, and dedication that made these programs possible largely materialized in towns such as El Segundo, Burbank, Downey, Canoga Park, and Huntington **Beach**.

Southern California's sunny climate, open land, top-notch universities, and tradition of entrepreneurship all helped to establish the region as a center for aerospace ventures. The local industry contributed to national defense projects throughout World War II and the Cold War, and by the 21st century, more than a half-million people were employed in more than 42,000 companies spread throughout every congressional and legislative district of the state. While several major companies have moved their operations to other regions, Southern California's aerospace assets remain critical to making the dreams of spaceflight a reality.

An Agave attenuata plant at the Huntington Botanical Gardens in San Marino, CA

AGAVE

Ah-GAH-veh Symmetrical, sculptural, and seemingly modern, agave plants grace Southern California with an exotic and sometimes Seussian air. Their gracefully tapered leaves grow in spiraling rosettes that shoot up a massive stalk of flowers, called an inflorescence. This magnificent display, which may take decades to produce, marks the end of the plant's life. Some species are called century plants because of the length of time it takes for the inflorescence to appear.

The *Agave* genus is an extensive collection of succulents that includes both the spiny and soft and the towering and tiny, all in shades of blues, greens, and grays. Some common varieties in Southern California include *Agave deserti*, a California native (most agaves are indigenous to Mexico); *Agave attenuata*, a soft-leafed agave with a tall and saggy flower stalk; and *Agave americana*, which, just before it blooms, resembles a giant asparagus. Aloes and yuccas, often confused with agaves, are of different genera.

Agave nectar, tequila, and mescal all come from agave plants, although these products typically hail from Mexico. The native inhabitants of Southern California once consumed agave stalks and flowers (which can still be found for sale in Latino markets). Fiber in the leaves was also used to make soap, sandals, and rope.

The 13-story Eastern Columbia Building (1930), which now houses condos, epitomizes Zig Zag Moderne style (a subgenre of Art Deco style) in downtown Los Angeles, CA

ART DECO STYLE

The name Art Deco comes from *L'Exposition Internationale des Arts Decoratifs et Industriels Modernes*, a showcase for art, architecture, and design held in Paris in 1925. Southern California adopted both variations of the style, Zig Zag Moderne (1925-1940) and Streamline Moderne (1930-1950), as popular design choices during their respective heydays. Zig Zag Moderne is vertically oriented (think skyscrapers) with angular, hard-edged forms and abstract ornamentation. Exotic materials, such as marble, terracotta, and terrazzo, placed on otherwise plain surfaces served to highlight this decoration. Streamline Moderne is horizontally oriented and utilizes less ornamentation. Classic Streamline Moderne buildings mimic the aerodynamism of automobile and aircraft design, with smooth walls, circular windows, and rounded edges.

Amid the countless Art Deco movie theaters, apartments, and government buildings scattered throughout the region, classic examples of the style include Los Angeles's Griffith Observatory (1934-1935), the former Bullock's Wilshire Department store (now the Southwestern Law School, 1929), and the Avalon Casino (1929) on Santa Catalina Island.

Like Miami and New York, the greater Los Angeles area is a treasure trove of Art Deco architecture, primarily because a huge growth spurt of the region coincided with the popularity of the style. Long Beach has many gems as well, having fallen victim to a major earthquake in 1933, which necessitated new building projects at the height of the Art Deco craze.

A ripe avocado from a heritage farm in Fillmore, CA

AVOCADO

Cloaked in thick canopies of dark green leaves, avocado (*Persea americana*) trees cling to California's cool mountain foothills from San Luis Obispo to San Diego. Along this 300-mile stretch, 6,800 growers cultivate about 90 percent of the nation's domestic crop. The different microclimates of the industry's two hubs, Santa Paula in Ventura County and Fallbrook in San Diego County, allow for harvest seasons throughout the year. Due to the fruit's high market value, farmers often resort to "guac cops" to thwart "grand theft avo" of their trees.

From sushi and salads to guacamole and **burgers**, avocados lend their buttery flavor and smooth texture to countless Californian dishes. This might be one reason that avocados are feasted upon in greater numbers in California than anywhere else in the nation. Although alligator pears, as they are also known, are native to Mexico, they are celebrated as locals at the annual Carpinteria and Fallbrook avocado festivals.

The state produces seven commercial avocado varieties, but the durable, dark-skinned Hass (rhymes with pass) is by far the most common. Hass avocados surpassed the arguably more flavorful Fuerte variety in volume about 50 years ago. Surprisingly, all Hass avocados can trace their lineage to one mother tree developed in the 1920s in La Habra Heights by a letter carrier named Rudolph Hass (1892–1952). *See also California Roll.*

An Oscar statue at the Dolby Theater is buffed and ready to greet the stars of the Academy Awards show in the Hollywood district of Los Angeles, CA

AWARD CEREMONY

What began in 1929 as an intimate banquet at Hollywood's Roosevelt Hotel has become an annual tradition to honor the best of the film industry. Although worlds away from the global, live-broadcast mega-event that it is today, the inaugural Academy Awards provided the template for the many award ceremonies that fill the calendars of the Hollywood elite.

The winter awards season is a busy one, with the Emmy (television industry), Golden Globe (television and motion picture), and Grammy (recording) award shows all leading up to the highly anticipated Oscars (motion picture). In between these major events are smaller shows presented by industry guilds and niche markets. Each show is a world unto itself, with quirky rituals and customs, most of which is unseen by television audiences. Some shows, such as the American Music Awards, reserve seating for the general public.

Award shows give the who's who of the entertainment world a night to hobnob with famous colleagues, stand in the limelight, and be their most glamorous. But when the red carpet rolls out, it isn't simply an excuse to party—winning is serious business in Tinseltown, which can equate to significant boosts for careers, audience numbers, and revenues. *See also Celebrity.*

A late 19th to early 20th century Mission Indian basket, probably Luiseño, made with sumac, juncus, and deergrass • Courtesy of the Southwest Museum of the American Indian Collection, Autry National Center, Los Angeles; 116.L.113

BASKETRY

Native cultures across Southern California—from the Chumash of Santa Barbara to the Kumeyaay of San Diego County—share a tradition of basketmaking that developed over thousands of years. After Spanish missionaries first made contact with indigenous peoples, baskets from the region collectively became known as **Mission** Indian style in the mid-1800s. These coiled receptacles played many roles in the daily lives of native peoples. Some were vessels for gathering, preparing, serving, and storing foods, while others were used for gifts, gambling, carrying babies, and rituals. From the 1930s through the 1950s rectangular Mission baskets woven by the Cahuilla tribe were used for shipping **dates** from the Coachella Valley.

The survival of this ancient craft depends on the mastery of multiple skills. Before weaving begins, artisans must locate, gather, and prepare the materials used in the weaving of a basket. This requires intimate knowledge of the landscape and may take months to achieve. Contemporary basket makers still favor three grasses—juncus (*Juncus textilis*), sumac (*Rhus trilobata*), and deer grass (*Muhlenbergia rigens*)—known for their strength, durability, and distinctive color and texture. Woven together, these materials help to create the striking designs for which these beautiful baskets are celebrated.

The evening sun begins its slow descent at Swami's State Beach in Encinitas, CA

BEACH

Southern California boasts more than 250 miles of Pacific coast. This magnificent shoreline features towering bluffs, hidden coves, protected **wetlands**, lagoons, tide pools, and sandy beaches. It is on these shores that California Cool evolved.

With more than 110 million annual visitors, and 90 percent of the region's residents living fewer than 100 miles from the coast, the beach is Southern California's favorite place for recreation. Bodybuilding, **surfing**, sunbathing, biking, fishing, skating, yachting, hang gliding, swimming, and volleyball all enjoy enthusiastic devotees. Moderate air and water temperatures allow for year-round activities, although Southern California beaches can be surprisingly chilly. A mix of cool offshore water, wind, and interior heat creates a foglike marine layer in coastal areas as well as the overcast and foggy weather of late spring known as May Gray and June Gloom.

Humans share coastal waters with brown pelicans, harbor seals, dolphins, **Pacific gray whales**, and even the odd great white shark. However, the risk of a Jaws attack is a lesser worry than the effects of pollution, runoff, overfishing, and climate change. The environmental advocacy group Heal the Bay helps to mitigate these threats through education and community action, including the Beach Report Card, which helps beachgoers determine when and where water pollution levels are safest. *See also Beach Cruiser, Grunion, Lifeguard Tower, Pacific Gray Whale, Pier, Surfing, and Wetland.*

Beach cruiser rentals are lined up and ready for a spin at Venice Bike and Skate in the Venice Beach neighborhood of Los Angeles, CA

BEACH CRUISER

When bike shop owner Larry Mc-Neely (1951–) tweaked a vintage bicycle clunker into a comfortable ride perfectly suited to the pathways that wind along California's shoreline, he named it a **beach** cruiser and started a phenomenon. This was during the mid-1970s in Newport Beach—a place that, like the rest of America, was inundated with foreign roadster bikes that featured lightweight framing, narrow tires, and the comfort of a sawhorse. Single-gear beach cruisers, with their wide seats, balloon tires, upright riding, and retro cool were a much better fit for the slow-paced beach community. Similar seaside towns, including Santa Monica and Venice, soon had legions of happy riders, and by the 1990s, most bike manufacturers offered a beach cruiser line. Similar to the world of **custom cars**, a thriving subculture evolved around the collection and personalization of cruiser bikes, both new and old.

Before cruisers enjoyed national fame, hard-core surfers and beach bums looked to the durability, practicality, and affordability of 1930s- to 1950s-era Schwinn bicycles, from which the beach cruiser evolved. With a few dollars at a garage sale and some fixing up, these bikes helped beachgoers get to the waves in comfort and style. And, with an added accessory rack, a surfboard could accompany the rider. Like a swimsuit and towel, the cruiser has become yet another item that typifies life at the beach. *See also Beach.*

Billboards compete for eyes on the Sunset Strip in West Hollywood, CA

BILLBOARD

Southern California's infamous traffic may be a headache for commuters, but it's an ideal opportunity for outdoor advertisers. The ability to reach a huge audience—largely motorists—for pennies on the dollar has made the billboard a ubiquitous feature of the landscape. Among the estimated 11,000 billboards in the Los Angeles area, the Sunset Strip in West Hollywood is the format's most prestigious locale, where hundreds of elevated advertisements dot the curvy thoroughfare.

To stand out from the competition, marketers have gone far beyond the traditional bulletin format (a 14-by-48-foot panel elevated on a metal post), turning to flashy digital billboards and supergraphics (oversize banners attached to building facades). The unattractive and distracting nature of this pervasive signage has the city of Los Angeles involved in an ongoing debate about the legality of this form of advertising.

Although the current monopoly of billboard usage seems to be for movies and television shows, some Angelenos remember a time when the city's billboard queen was a busty model and actress known as Angelyne. Using pink cursive script for slogans such as "Barbie wishes she were me," Angelyne's unabashed self-promotion gained her **celebrity** status in Hollywood, further promoting the myth that anything is possible in Tinseltown. *See also Freeway.*

With several shelves of elixirs behind him, an Indian spirit guide welcomes visitors to El Indio Amazonico Botanica in downtown Los Angeles, CA

BOTANICA

Although easy to overlook and hard to figure out (at least for the uninitiated), botanicas are indispensable cultural resources and sites of healing for many communities. Found primarily in Latino neighborhoods, these mom-and-pop shops are mini-marts of religious merchandise, herbs, objects of devotion, spiritual guidance, and mystical intervention.

Botanicas arrived in Southern California in the 1950s by way of Cuban immigrants and represent the traditions of the region's pan-Latino diaspora for a unique blending of Santería, Catholicism, Espiritismo, and Curanderismo (folk healing). A typical botanica visually exemplifies this spiritual mash-up with floor-to-ceiling displays of herbal packages, amulets, candles, and altars. Merchandise is intermixed with an assortment of spiritual effigies, including Native American spirit guides, Buddhas, San Simón (a Guatemalan folk spirit), Niño Dios (baby Jesus), and the **Virgin of Guadalupe**.

Whether serving a customer who is a newly arrived immigrant in need of legal counsel, a follwer of Santería requiring a *limpia* (spiritual cleansing), or a second-generation housewife seeking the soothing comforts of her grandmother's herbal elixirs, botanicas are culturally appropriate alternatives to the church, pharmacy, and community center, providing their diverse clientele healing for the body, mind, and spirit.

Abundant bougainvillea lines the walkways at the Beverly Hills Hotel in Beverly Hills, CA

BOUGAINVILLEA

Boo-guhn-VIL-ee-uh Like Florida, Arizona, South Carolina, Louisiana, and Hawaii, Southern California is a hotbed for a vibrant flowering vine called bougainvillea. This native of South America was named after the French navigator Louis Antoine de Bougainville (1729–1811), who claimed that his first acquaintance with the plant, in Brazil, was one of the highlights of his voyage around the world.

Southern California is particularly well suited to bougainvillea, which adds a romantic flair to the plain stucco walls of the region's **Mission**-inspired architecture. The plant thrives in Mediterranean climates worldwide, adding striking magenta, pink, scarlet, yellow, and coral hues to the fences, walls, and columns it climbs. Its signature burst of color comes from the papery, pollinator-attracting bracts, which engulf small, inconspicuous white flowers. Local horticulturalists have added many intensely hued hybrids to the long list of bougainvillea varieties available, including California Gold and San Diego Red.

At least four cities in Southern California—Laguna Niguel, San Clemente, La Mesa, and Camarillo—claim bougainvilleas as their official flower. However, nowhere has the plant grown so profusely as one vine in Glendora that stretches 600 feet along two avenues. The Glendora bougainvillea is the largest such plant in the United States and became the city's first state Historical Landmark in 1978.

A California burrito at a strip mall eatery in San Clemente, CA

BURRITO

As complete meals that can be eaten on the go, burritos are a go-to food for everyone, from hungry hipsters to those nursing a hangover. While burritos originated in Mexican cuisine, local varieties are strictly a north-of-the-border phenomenon. Like so many Americanized versions of ethnic food, Southern California's "little donkeys" (burrito is a diminutive of *burro*, Spanish for donkey) are often not so little.

In San Diego the California burrito is king. This regional favorite is made with a wheat tortilla wrapped around *carne asada* (thin strips of grilled beef), loads of cheese, french fries, and a combination of *pico de gallo* (a condiment of fresh tomatoes, onions, and chilies), sour cream, and guacamole. Carne asada fries, another beloved San Diego creation, are a cousin to this dish, lacking only the tortilla and salsa.

Heading northward, burritos simplify, shrink, and standardize. Angelenos typically find their fix of refried beans, cheese, and stewed meat at taquerías and even **burger** joints. While the two cities may quibble over which is best, nothing overshadows the bitter dispute between SoCal and NorCal, where obsessive fever for the enormous **mission**-style burrito runs high. If used as a weapon, these cylindrical bricks of tinfoil-wrapped black beans, meat, rice, and more would easily demolish any rival. But might isn't always right, is it?

Dessert options at Clifton's Cafeteria (pre-remodel) in downtown Los Angeles, CA

CAFETERIA

Amid downtown Los Angeles's crumbling **movie palaces** and ghetto-chic clothing stalls stands Clifton's Brookdale Cafeteria, one of the last cafeterias of the golden age. Unlike the institutional ambiance and bland flavors that such establishments are known for today, cafeterias were *the* place to eat from the early 1900s through the 1950s. Informality, affordability, and choice reeled customers in, but these thriving establishments also offered grand spaces, delectable meals, and a flourishing social scene. Behind many of the establishments that turned 1920s Southern California into "Sunny Cafeteria," as writer Harry Leon Wilson (1867–1939) termed it, were three influential restaurateurs: the Boos brothers, who helped to popularize the concept; Alfred Schaber (1893–1962), who started the Schaber's Cafeteria chain; and Clifford Clifton (1900–1969), remembered for his kitschy-themed interiors and free meals for the hungry during the Depression.

Some historians surmise that cafeterias were so successful in Los Angeles because they offered hearty home cooking and a place to gather for the hordes of homesick Midwesterners who helped transform the dusty desert pueblo into the bustling megalopolis it has become. However, when automobiles became the favored mode of transportation after World War II, drive-through dining and fast-food stands quickly replaced these self-service restaurants.

A walking calavera takes part in Reyes Rodriguez's Calavera Fashion Show at Tropico de Nopal Gallery and Art Space in Los Angeles, CA

CALAVERA

Kala-VEHR-ah The *calavera* (Spanish for skull) is a potent symbol for Chicanos and Mexicans, who have roots in ancient Aztec civilization. Imbued with dynamism and character, contemporary renditions are almost wholly inspired by the satirical posters of the Mexican printmaker José Guadalupe Posada (1852–1913). The legendary Angeleno **graffiti** artist Chaz Bojorquez (1949–) may be the Posada of our time, having invented a late 1960s-era calavera persona known as Señor Suerte (Mr. Luck). An icon of the Highland Park Avenues gang, Señor Suerte is characterized by a fedora, a fur coat, a sardonic smile, and crossed fingers. Around the same time Señor Suerte first appeared, the burgeoning Chicano movement began using the skull image to reclaim cultural heritage and ethnic pride. Calaveras are evident in a variety of creative expressions, including graffiti, tattoos, paintings, lowrider imagery, and Dia de Los Muertos (Day of the Dead) celebrations.

Day of the Dead is celebrated on November 1 and 2 to honor departed souls. A joyous occasion, it features processions, dancing, traditional foods, and decorated *ofrendas* (altars). Self-Help Graphics in East Los Angeles hosted the nation's first free public Day of the Dead event in 1973, and the custom continues today. Olvera Street and Hollywood Forever Cemetery also organize notable renditions of the holiday. *See also Graffiti.*

A cozy bungalow retreat in the historic Bungalow Heaven neighborhood of Pasadena, CA

CALIFORNIA BUNGALOW

At the turn of the 20th century, bungalow homes answered the call for affordable housing for middle-class families. First introduced on the East Coast and derived from the low, gabled *bangla* homes in Bengali, the bungalow was the predominant type of housing up until the Great Depression in California. The distinctive horizontal massing, low pitched, gabled roofs (often with overhanging eaves), and ample porches became so entangled with the look of the state's residential architecture that these homes became known as California bungalows, regardless of where they were built. Pasadena, Riverside, Claremont, Long **Beach**, and Los Angeles still contain large concentrations of these quaint structures.

The term *bungalow* refers to a type of home—modest, simplified one- to one-and-a-half-story houses with airy interiors and gardens—and not a specific style. They could be rendered in the **Spanish Colonial Revival style**, for instance, but were most commonly made as Craftsman homes. This fashion was part of the Arts and Crafts movement, which espoused fine craftsmanship, the use of high quality materials, and the direct expression of structure—the antithesis of the rich ornamentation characterized by the preceding Victorian era. The Pasadena architecture firm Greene and Greene was a proponent of the Craftsman sensibility, and the pair elevated the style with lavish Ultimate Bungalows, of which the Gamble House (1908) in Pasadena is a prime example.

A golden carpet of California poppies grace the hills just outside the Antelope Valley California Poppy Reserve in Lancaster, CA

CALIFORNIA POPPY

Drought-tolerant, self-seeding, and easy to grow, the California poppy (*Eschscholzia californica*) is a standout. The drama of the blooms is found not in their form, but in their fiery burst of color, most magnificently expressed in multitudes. The flower's bright orange petals evoke the Golden State's seemingly eternal sunshine, optimism, and abundance, making it the perfect choice for the state flower. Poppies are woven into the very history of California through the legends of native tribes, Spanish conquistadors, and 49ers. Spanish explorers could reportedly see "rivers of gold" on the foothills of the San Gabriel Mountains from their ships at sea. This area became the San Pasqual Rancho, which in-cluded present-day Pasadena, Altadena, and Sierra Madre. The vibrant carpets of color once found there were known as *La Sabanilla de San Pasqual* (the altar cloth of Saint Pascal), referring to the shepherd saint who communed with God in a field of wildflowers.

Before these vast fields were plowed for housing, picnics among the blossoms were a springtime ritual in Southern California, much like cherry blossom gazing in Japan. Today the only large poppy fields left are at the Antelope Valley Poppy Reserve near Lancaster. The area is blanketed in gold at the peak of blooming season, which usually occurs around April 6, also known as California Poppy Day.

A classic pitcher from the Bauer Pottery Company of Glendale, CA

CALIFORNIA POTTERY

From the 1930s to the 1950s Southern California was alive with pottery makers. In 1948, the peak year for the industry, more than 800 companies in the state were churning out figurines, tableware, tile, and decorative housewares to meet national demand. Especially popular were simple earthenware dishes with bright, solid-color glazing, a signature style of the region. Bauer Pottery, Brayton Laguna, and Catalina Clay are generally credited with initiating this modern take on a centuries-old craft.

The foundation of California pottery lies in the **decorative tiles** used to embellish the **Spanish Colonial Revival** dwellings of the early 1900s. This legacy, along with locally available raw materials—clay, talc, and natural gas for kiln fuel—made the region attractive for similar clay-based businesses. Unlike other industries, potteries prospered during the Great Depression and World War II, buoyed by the wealth of the thriving motion picture industry and the wartime ban on imports. But ultimately, it was Southern California's unique tradition of outdoor living that allowed the simple, informal designs to flourish.

The big five—Bauer, Pacific, Gladding-McBean, Metlox, and Vernon—mass-produced most of the region's ceramics, although many smaller studios contributed significantly to this local specialty. Cheap imports from Japan and Italy halted production in the early 1950s, leaving only a handful of companies remaining today. *See also Decorative Tile.*

A late 1960s ranch house in Beverly Hills, CA

CALIFORNIA RANCH HOUSE

After World War II, Americans were hungry for a new approach to family living. Years of wartime sacrifice fed the desire for a more carefree existence and an interest in updating homes with new technologies. The rise of automobile ownership allowed families to move to neighborhoods with sprawling lots where low-slung, rambling abodes with open floor plans and light-filled spaces could be built. The resulting ranch house, America's first widely available Modern shelter, had arrived.

Architect Cliff May (1908–1989), largely recognized as the father of the California ranch house, found inspiration in the state's 19th-century Hispanic *rancheros*—one-story structures with a horizontal emphasis, low-pitched roofs, and rectangular U- or L-shaped footprints. His use of patios, expansive glass, and sliding doors emphasized openness and outdoor living, which allowed residents to enjoy Southern California's benign climate. **Bungalow** homes, with their flexibility, breakdown of formal space, and lack of pretense, also influenced the designs that defined the ranch as a symbol of the casual western lifestyle.

The first ranch homes appeared in the 1930s, but the genre's popularity peaked as the nation's preeminent postwar housing solution, especially throughout Orange County and the San Gabriel and San Fernando Valleys. The style faded in the 1970s, but the inescapable ranch house endures as the embodiment of Southern California's easy living. *See also California Bungalow.*

A California roll from a sushi restaurant in Mission Hills, CA

CALIFORNIA ROLL

At the turn of the 20th century, Japanese immigrants provided major advancements to Southern California's developing fishing and agricultural industries. But perhaps Japan's most enduring mark on American culture is sushi. The unique culinary custom of topping vinegared rice with raw seafood arrived in North America in the 1960s. The novelty wasn't accepted wholeheartedly until Ichiro Mashita (1935–), a chef at Los Angeles's downtown Tokyo Kaikan restaurant, created a palatable alternative in the 1970s. Using cooked crab, **avocado**, and cucumbers, Mashita successfully concealed some potentially unsavory aspects of the Japanese staple from the Western palate. The oily texture of avocado makes a sublime substitution for *toro*

(fatty tuna), and the roll is formed inside out so that the seaweed wrap is hidden by an outer layer of steamed rice and toasted sesame seeds. While hardliners consider the California roll to be sushi-lite, it is widely credited with fueling the popularity of sushi worldwide.

Unfettered by tradition, sushi chefs have flourished in the Southern California since the introduction of the California roll, filling entire menus with similarly unconventional *maki-zushi* (rolled sushi) concoctions. Thanks to its embrace of fusion dishes and proximity to Asia, the area remains a fertile environment for inventive sushi chefs, influential sushi bars, and some of the finest sushi dining outside Japan.

Case Study House #8 (1949), the iconic home of designers Ray and Charles Eames, in the Pacific Palisades neighborhood of Los Angeles, CA

CASE STUDY HOUSE

In 1945 the editor of *Arts & Architecture* magazine, John Entenza (1906–1984), began the Case Study House Program, which pioneered some of the most influential works of midcentury architecture. This visionary initiative allowed architects to experiment with new materials and techniques, most of which emerged from World War II-era technologies, to produce models of efficient, low-cost, modern housing for the average American family.

The participating architects were Modernists, ranging from the internationally recognized Richard Neutra (1892–1970) and Pierre Koenig (1925–2004) to local luminaries such as Whitney R. Smith (1911–2002). Using donated materials, each architect was asked to design and construct a home for the new era. The public was invited to visit each finished dwelling, and the results were published alongside iconic black-and-white photographs by Julius Shulman (1910–2009) in *Arts & Architecture* magazine.

When it ended in 1966, the Case Study House Program had produced 36 prototypes, most of which were built in and around Los Angeles. Although nearly a dozen remain only as blueprints, Case Study houses are viewed as monumental works, having succeeded in introducing countless innovations to American home builders, including the blending of indoor and outdoor spaces, sliding glass doors, prefabrication techniques, open floor plans, and steel framing. *See also Modern Architecture.*

A celebrity devotee polishes the star of silent movie actress Louise Glaum on the Hollywood Walk of Fame in the Hollywood district of Los Angeles, CA

CELEBRITY

In this land where fantasy reigns, celebrities are demigods: their footprints are immortalized in cement, their names grace public parks, streets, and airports, and their presence can incite instant paparazzi mobs.

Most celebrities are the creations of Hollywood, the Entertainment Capital of the World, where they are honored on more than 2,400 stars on the Hollywood Walk of Fame for their achievements in television, film, radio, music, and theater. Of course, only a tiny percentage of entertainers ever attain such financial and professional success, and for those who do, constant public scrutiny becomes a fact of daily life.

Long before Twitter and *People* magazine, feeding the public's hunger for celebrity news was an imperative in the making of a star. At the turn of the 20th century, when actors were not listed in credits, performers believed a movie connection would ruin their theater careers, and producers feared actors would gain too much power. But the public demanded to know the names of the stars, and they proved to be loyal to their favorites. Legendary Universal Pictures producer Carl Laemmle (1867–1939) lassoed this fascination and manufactured the first movie stars in his "star system." His groundbreaking use of media manipulation, heavy promotion, and contractual control helped pave the way for today's celebrity culture. *See also Studio Lot.*

A section of Griffith Park flaunts its subtle spring colors in Los Angeles, CA

CHAPARRAL

Chaparral is one of the most common types of vegetation in Southern California and an integral part of the region's natural heritage. Because chaparral has played a supporting role in countless Western movies, television shows, and commercials, its evergreen trees and hardy scrub are familiar even to those who have never stepped foot in the state.

The name for this group of drought-tolerant and fire-hardy plants comes from the Spanish word for a dwarf evergreen **oak** tree, *chaparra*. The harsh terrain necessitated leather protective wear for cowboys that became known as *chaps*. Common chaparral greenery includes chamise, ceanothus, sagebrush, manzanita, sumac, mesquite, and buckwheat. These form a dense and prickly playground for the diverse animals, birds, insects, and reptiles that make it their home. Another widespread shrub, the red-berried *toyon* (*Heteromeles arbutifolia*), or California holly, is the namesake of Hollywood.

Covering approximately seven million acres of foothills and mountainsides from Catalina Island to the eastern deserts and from Oregon to Baja California, the deep green hues of chaparral offer respite from SoCal's concrete expanses. But as humans inch into this native terrain, they risk exposure to an integral component of the chaparral's ecology—fire. Like the spectacular fire annuals—wildflowers that appear only in the specialized conditions following a blaze—chaparral vegetation depends on the ravages of flame for its renewal and rebirth. *See also Oak and Wildfire.*

Chips and three styles of salsa are served before a meal of tacos and tamales in Santa Monica, CA

CHIPS AND SALSA

Chips and salsa, the ubiquitous appetizer found at taco stands, Mexican restaurants, and countless backyard parties, is a relatively recent combination of old and new customs. Salsa, an important element of ancient Aztec cuisine, has evolved into a mix of ingredients indigenous to the Old World (onions, garlic, and vinegar) and the New (chilies, tomatillos, and tomatoes). Once exclusive to areas with primarily Hispanic populations, salsa has become a favorite American condiment, outselling ketchup, at least in revenue, since the early 1990s. A wide variety of styles are served throughout Southern California—from chunky to thin, from mild to rip-roaring hot. Red salsa has a tomato base; green salsa (also called *verde* sauce) is made with tomatillos.

Tortilla chips are a more recent invention. Although fried tortillas were sometimes eaten as snacks in Mexico, their large-scale production can be traced to the frying up of excess *masa* (corn dough) at a masa mill in San Antonio, Texas around 1919. The more persistent legend, however, credits Rebecca Webb Carranza (1908–2006) of East Los Angeles as the inventor of "Tort Chips," made from the misshapen tortillas of her tortilla factory in the late 1940s. Some 40 years later, the Tortilla Industry Association awarded her the Golden Tortilla for the innovation.

As *chilaquiles,* tortilla chips become a meal in themselves. This Mexican-style breakfast is made with salsa-drenched chips fried up with onions, eggs, cheese, and topped with sour cream.

Dancy tangerines ripen on a tree at the E. Waldo Ward & Sons Orchard in Sierra Madre, CA

CITRUS FRUIT

California's gold rush of 1849 coincided with a gold rush of another kind: citrus fruits. The state's first commercial orchard was planted in 1840 with seeds from the local Spanish **mission** in what is now downtown Los Angeles. Although fruit provided sustenance and vitamin C to scurvy-prone miners, these oranges were small and bitter. To counter these issues, an orchard owner developed the Valencia variety, a summer hybrid known for its juiciness, color, and tough skin.

It was a winter variety, the navel orange, that eventually made the citrus industry a major economic and social force in the state. In 1873 Brazilian cuttings were sent to Riverside resident Eliza Tibbets (1823–1898) to determine if navels could be successful in California. There was no question—by 1893 Riverside had the nation's highest wealth per capita, thanks to citrus crops. A prosperous citrus belt grew across the inland foothills of the San Gabriel and San Bernardino Mountains as well as in Orange County. Postcard pictures of snow-capped mountains behind pretty golden fruits encouraged the winter weary to think of Southern California as a tropical paradise.

While most of these heritage orchards were plowed over after World War II to make room for suburban developments, nearly three-fourths of the nation's fresh citrus crop is still grown in the state, mostly in the Central Valley.

The Laugh Factory Comedy Club stage awaits the next comic in the Hollywood district of Los Angeles, CA

COMEDY CLUB

Comedy clubs are intimate venues where working comedians perform, workshop, and showcase their acts. The oldest in the country, Pasadena's Ice House, which opened in 1960 when most clubs catered to folk music acts, led the way for the comedy boom that arrived in the 1970s.

By presenting several acts a night, comedy clubs inadvertently supported a growing community of comedians who could experiment with their acts, network, and provide feedback to each other. The comedy world officially shifted to the Golden State from New York and Las Vegas when Johnny Carson (1925–2005) moved *The Tonight Show* to "beautiful downtown Burbank" in 1972.

Graduates of the Los Angeles comedy scene include Tim Allen, Roseanne Barr, George Carlin, Jim Carrey, Dana Carvey (holding the record for most standing ovations at the Icehouse), Bill Cosby, Billy Crystal, Ellen DeGeneres, David Letterman, Steve Martin, Bob Newhart, Jerry Seinfeld, Lily Tomlin, and Robin Williams. With this track record, comedy clubs are rich scouting grounds for the next generation of talent.

Playing off the region's great tradition of entertainment, comedy is a booming business with its heart in Hollywood. Superb standup, improv, and sketch comedy acts are showcased nightly in storied institutions such as the Comedy Store, the Groundling Theater, the Improv, and Upright Citizens Brigade, confirming that Southern California is a vibrant and influential center of American humor.

A lowrider and its owner wait in a lot until they are needed for a film shoot in downtown Los Angeles, CA

CUSTOM CAR

In a land created, quite literally, for cars, status is closely tied to ownership—the more the better—and a black BMW is a typical starting point to making an impression. Rarer, pricier, and faster models will further raise eyebrows, but the ultimate cool is achieved with a custom ride.

Southern California largely supports and supplies the $30 billion custom car industry, which began as a local fad in the 1930s. Old cars were stripped of unnecessary parts, chopped, and elevated to hot rod status. When World War II servicemen returned home with machinery skills, the need for speed became a national obsession. Dry lakes in the Mojave Desert provided a uniform surface for racing, which later moved onto any available flat path. Aesthetics eventually overtook speed, and car bodies turned into metal canvases for individual expression. Chicanos invented a distinct identity by lowering their suspensions to devise lowriders, which evolved to include sophisticated hydraulics, detailed interiors, and candy-colored paint jobs.

Whether the goal is fast and furious or low and slow, customization has expanded into whole lifestyles of Kustom Kulture, each with its own music, fashion, artwork, and slang. Enthusiasts abound at the regular rallies, rides, and cruise nights held in nearly every SoCal city with a long enough drag or a big enough parking lot.

Farm workers harvest some of the last Barhi dates of the season (bunches are covered with protective paper) in Indio, CA

DATE

Dates are the soft and chewy fruit of the date palm (*Phoenix datylifera*). Introduced in California by Spanish missionaries in the late 1700s, dates began to be cultivated 200 years later, after the United States Department of Agriculture assessed the area's growing conditions using imported palm offshoots. Success in the Coachella Valley (roughly 120 miles east of Los Angeles) proved that the area maintained the necessary prolonged high heat and low humidity that date palms require to produce high-quality fruit. Today 95 percent of the nation's dates are grown there.

Date farming is a labor-intensive and expensive endeavor, requiring continual care and irrigation. The **palm trees** must be manually detho-rned and pollinated, and the date bunches must be thinned and covered to protect them from rain and pests. Fruit pickers use permanent ladders attached to each tree during harvest time, which lasts from late summer through midwinter.

Each February a date festival in Indio celebrates the harvest and honors the fruit's Middle Eastern roots with date judging, Arabian dances, and camel races. But date farms welcome visitors year-round to try a seemingly endless variety of dates, and creamy date shakes too. Among the popular stops is Indio's Shields Date Garden, where the curious can watch a presentation called *The Romance and Sex Life of the Date.*

The elaborate fountain and ocean view at the historic Adamson House and Malibu Lagoon Museum (former site of Malibu Potteries) in Malibu, CA

DECORATIVE TILE

California vintage tile is inextricable from the state's distinctive architectural heritage and style. Fountains, fireplace mantels, stair risers, flooring, and countertops all lend themselves to bright splashes of color and festive patterning. Depictions of regional wildlife and history also add charm and romance to the red-tiled and stuccoed buildings they adorn.

Californians were introduced to locally made tile in the lavishly decorated buildings of the 1915 Panama–California Exposition; such ornamentation has been a fixture in **Spanish Colonial Revival** architecture ever since. Tile making closely aligned with the popularity of this architectural style, and both reached their peak in the 1920s.

Like most local potteries, the short-lived but highly influential Malibu Tile Company (1926–32) utilized locally sourced clay that was hand-crafted and painted with rich glazes. While many companies were known for elaborate abstract patterning inspired by Moorish, Spanish, and Andalusian motifs, a few created designs more suited to Arts and Crafts–style homes. Such tiles featured rustic reliefs and subdued palettes, such as the work of Pasadena-based Ernest Batchelder (1875–1957).

Most early-20th-century California tile is behind closed doors in private homes. However, Los Angeles's Union Station, Malibu's Adamson House, Santa Barbara's Courthouse, and Catalina Island's town of Avalon are all publicly accessible showcases for this charming regional craft. *See also California Pottery.*

A resident desert tortoise charges the camera at the Moorten Botanical Gardens in Palm Springs, CA

DESERT TORTOISE

The desert tortoise (*Gopherus agassizii*) is California's official reptile, and in many ways they are exemplary residents of the state. Tortoises are experts at conserving water (they can go without drinking for more than a year), have learned how to survive the desert heat (they sleep through most of the spring and summer), and eat plenty of healthy greens, including grasses, cacti, herbs, and desert blossoms. Their only un-Californian trait is their extremely slow speed of locomotion (never seen on a SoCal **freeway)**, which clocks in at an average 0.2 miles per hour. Perhaps taking it easy has something to do with their longevity—the species is estimated to have existed for 15 to 20 million years, with a lifespan of up to 100 years.

The washes and canyons of the Mojave and Sonoran Deserts are the perfect habitat for these creatures, offering plenty of burrowing opportunities in dry, sandy soil. The reptiles spend up to 95 percent of their time underground, conserving their energy and escaping extreme temperatures as well as prey. Nonetheless, the demolition of the tortoise's natural habitat is one of the greatest hazards to the animals, which are listed as "threatened" on the California and Federal Endangered Species Lists.

A classic dingbat apartment on Hayworth Street in Hollywood, CA

DINGBAT APARTMENT

Simultaneously admired for retro-kitsch styling and despised for cheap construction, the dingbat apartment building personifies the best of Southern California's inventive exuberance and the worst of its short-term thinking. In the 1950s and 1960s these boxy two- to three-story walk-ups replaced Victorian, Craftsman, and **Spanish Colonial Revival** homes in established neighborhoods throughout the region. With individual entrances that open to the outside, garden courtyards, and on-site parking tucked under second-story rooms, dingbats offered throngs of postwar renters an alternative to tenement-style living and a semblance of home ownership. For property owners, dingbats were economic no-brainers—the high-density and relatively cheap structures offered more rent for a low cost.

Even at their most basic, dingbat apartments always matched or even exceeded the style of their time, mimicking elements of Modernism, **Googie** architecture, and even the pastel color themes of 1950s consumer products. Playful fixtures, abstract ornamentation, and glorified names such as Kenmore Tropics and Capri Villa coated these simple stucco boxes with an alluring glamour and mystique that still charms admirers of these aging relics.

Uplifted rock formations showcase the power of seismic activity along the San Andreas Fault at Vasquez Rocks Natural Area Park near Agua Dulce, CA

EARTHQUAKE

From Cape Mendocino southwest to the Salton Sea lies the San Andreas fault, an 800-mile zone of fractures in the earth's crust. This is where the North American plate (which includes most of North America) and the Pacific plate (which includes parts of coastal California and most of the Pacific Ocean) push against each other in one of the few sites on the planet where an active fault occurs on land. The 70-mile-thick plates shift about 2 inches per year, with coastal Southern California heading northwest toward San Francisco and the larger landmass moving southeast. Of the hundreds of faults in the state, the San Andreas is by far the largest and most active.

Up to 30 quakes a day occur in the Southern California, most of which are barely felt by residents, if at all. However, catastrophic tremblors, some of which are felt hundreds of miles away, have besieged the area for millennia. In recent history, massive quakes in Southern California have been registered in Fort Tejon (in 1857, estimated magnitude: 8.0), Long **Beach** (1933: 6.3), Sylmar (1971: 6.6), and Northridge (1994: 6.7). Scientists predict that another Big One, measuring 8.0 or greater, is imminent, but the question of when remains unanswered.

Wind turbines along Interstate 10 in San Gorgonio Pass outside Palm Springs, CA

ENERGY FARM

With an abundance of natural resources, unique geography, and a history of political support, Southern California is a national leader in renewable-energy farming. Solar, wind, geothermal, biomass, and small hydroelectric facilities make up 12 percent of the state's electricity needs; another 9 percent comes from large hydroelectric plants. These numbers will continue to rise as California law requires state utilities to increase their use of renewables to 33 percent by 2020.

Concerns about fossil-fuel dependency (following the 1970s **oil** crisis), tax incentives, and the 1998 utilities deregulation all helped to establish solar and wind farms across California. Some of the most visible of these include the San Gorgonio Pass wind farms, composed of more than 4,000 wind turbines in a 70-square-mile area outside Palm Springs. Developed in the 1980s to capture some of the most reliable winds in the region (averaging 15–20 miles per hour), these were some of the nation's first wind turbines. Westward-moving Santa Ana winds blow from March to September, coinciding with peak summer energy demands.

California's wind capacity is currently more than twice that of solar, but the state is also a pioneer in harnessing the sun's energy. The popularity of rooftop solar panels is surging, as are sprawling commercial farms, some of which cover desert acreage so enormous that they glitter when photographed from space.

A eucalyptus tree reaching heavenward in Montecito, CA

EUCALYPTUS

Tall, with long, slender leaves, the aromatic eucalyptus (*Eucalyptus globulus*) graces the valleys, plains, and hills of Southern California. Australian miners introduced their "blue gum" trees during the California gold rush to provide prospectors with fuel, timber, shade, and beauty. Although the region had native willow, sycamore, and **oak** trees, numerous accounts described a "treeless" land "destitute of timber." The planting of rapid-growing eucalyptus was considered the solution to this problem.

The first saplings were planted in San Francisco in the early 1850s, and they appeared in Southern California about a decade later. By the turn of the 20th century a eucalyptus boom was under way. Proponents claimed the tree could provide shelter from the wind, increase rainfall, clean the air, provide a cash crop of medicinal oil and timber, and even turn the landscape into "the paradise of the world," according to Ellwood Cooper (1829–1918), a Santa Barbara rancher and eucalyptus booster. With the help of government programs, countless farmers furiously covered their acreage with eucalypti. Enthusiasm turned to disdain, however, as investors realized young growth made poor hardwood for the durable ties that railroad companies sought. Many of these eucalyptus groves were later subdivided into country estates.

Although considered an invasive species, the trees soften the landscape and form excellent windbreaks. By 1950, 2,000 miles of eucalyptus protected countless **citrus** orchards, as they still do today.

The Citadel Outlets (1930), a former tire manufacturing factory modeled after Dur-Sharrukin, the 7th century BC Assyrian Palace of King Sargon II, in Commerce, CA

FANTASY ARCHITECTURE

Buildings rendered to resemble streamliner ships, medieval castles, and Dutch windmills are just some of the quirky examples of architecture that has characterized notable structures throughout the Southern California since the turn of the 20th century. Fantasy architecture was the extreme end of a craze for period revival styles that reached its peak in the 1920s. Especially in Hollywood, where the line between fantasy and reality is often blurred, residential streets read like the pages of a catalogue for historic buildings, with Norman châteaus, Tudor cottages, and Egyptian Revival **bungalows**. Some enthusiastic designers took these notions even further, creating elaborate Hindu temples or Mayan palaces, many of which have become beloved landmarks.

Two factors that fueled this exuberance for the unconventional are a populace characterized by impermanency and the influence of the motion picture industry. Without the suppressing opinion of friends and relatives, newcomers to the region found the courage to construct their fantasies. With the technical ability and exotic repertoires of Hollywood's movie-set makers, their dreams could be made real.

Inspiration came from the slew of period films of the 1920s, including the biblical epic *The Ten Commandments* by Cecil B. DeMille (1881–1959). Flamboyant Hollywood stars added to Hollywoodland's eccentric streak, demanding capricious homes to reflect their theatrical profession. *See also Programmatic Architecure, Tiki Culture, and Visionary Environment.*

A bounty of produce for sale at the Santa Monica Farmers' Market in Santa Monica, CA

FARMERS' MARKET

When fresh, local produce is available daily at farmers' markets from Santa Barbara to San Diego, it is difficult to imagine that just 30 years ago these public marketplaces were nearly nonexistent. In 1979 six farmers engendered a historic change in food distribution by offering their harvests to the public in a Gardena parking lot. The highly successful event spawned hundreds of similar markets across the region (and later nationwide). Not only did they vastly improve access to fresh produce, farmers' markets eased the tremendous economic squeeze that regulations, corporate farming, and low prices had created for small farmers.

Today farmers' markets are hugely popular. Most municipalities have at least one local market that supplies an array of treats—from heirloom carrots to handmade preserves—that beautifully showcase the area's agricultural abundance and diversity. In addition to regional staples, shoppers can find local specialties such as Ojai Pixie tangerines, cherimoyas, cactus fruits, and Coachella Valley **dates**.

Los Angeles County alone has more than 100 weekly markets, and has announced plans to become the farmers' market capital of the world. Along with the flourishing markets in Hollywood and Santa Monica, where top chefs of the area source foodstuffs for their restaurants, the county hosts more than 1,000 farmers who sell to 250,000 weekly shoppers. *See also Citrus Fruit and Strawberry Field.*

An In-N-Out Burger sign beckons travelers to the beloved fast-food chain in Fountain Valley, CA

FAST-FOOD BURGER

SoCal put the fast in fast-food, and it all started with the burger. The growth of car culture played a major role in the evolution of the region's famous fare, from the German "hamburg steak" first seen in San Fernando in 1871 to the whip-quick sandwich burger we know today. In the 1930s drive-up barbecue stands began emerging as meeting places for teens, including the first McDonald's, which opened in San Bernardino in 1940. The owners quickly recognized that the food was often cold by the time it was delivered by carhop and that burgers were more profitable than barbecue. McDonald's reorganized their operations, and in 1948 the restaurant's short-order cooks and complex menu were replaced by unskilled workers who assembled simplified burgers with production-line efficiency. The model became famous, with restaurateurs flying in just to witness this revolutionary Speedee Service System.

Soon the postwar masses could choose from many McDonald's locations (the oldest operating franchise is a historic monument in Downey), as well as the San Diego-born Jack in the Box (1951) and Irvine-based In-N-Out Burger, which introduced the nation's first drive-through restaurant in 1948. It's not uncommon to see Californians, as in love with their cars as they were in the 1950s, waiting in long drive-through lines even when the counter is line free, all for the pleasure of a good burger. *See also Googie Style, Hot Dog, and Pastrami.*

A film location sign (in yellow) marks crew parking for a commercial being filmed in the Hollywood district of Los Angeles, CA

FILM LOCATION SIGN

They can be spotted on virtually any street across Los Angeles—bright yellow signs with clear black lettering that point to the on-site locations for Hollywood's commercials, films, and television shows. Crew members follow these markers to the sets, which are identified by words or phrases corresponding to a shoot. Secret codes—such as "Magnus Rex," which was used for "The Dark Knight Rises"—are sometimes used to keep **celebrity**-seekers from finding the film set.

The location department for each production determines the best site to shoot each scene and is also in charge of placing and taking down these signs. Every location must pass a laundry list of considerations: Will extraneous sounds be a problem? Can a film permit be obtained? Is there ample parking? Can the site provide the needed wattage? Is the space large enough to accommodate the crew? Finally, and perhaps number one in the minds of the producers, does the location fee fit the budget?

Increasingly, cost is a crucial issue for the motion picture industry. Many other states, such as New Mexico, Louisiana, New York, and Illinois, are sporting the same telltale signs of a film shoot in progress due to their competitive tax breaks, supportive **studio** complexes, versatile locations, and local film crews. *See also Studio Lot.*

Colorful Tecolote Giant ranunculus flowers at The Flower Fields in Carlsbad, CA

FLOWER FARM

From foothills awash in **California poppies** to Pasadena's Tournament of Roses, Southern California's history has long been tangled up with flowers. As the national leader in the billion-dollar industry of flower farming, the state continues its primacy. The temperate climate of Southern California's coastal regions makes it ideal for farmers to cultivate a wide range of beautiful blooms for ornament, cut flowers, and seed production.

A quarter of the state's flower farms are in San Diego County, including the Tecolote Giant ranunculus-covered Flower Fields in Carlsbad. The area, including nearby Encinitas and Leucadia, was once awash in blooms, but like other areas, urbanization is edging out agricultural land. In northwest Orange County, greenhouse-grown ornamental plants are another floral fixture, while Santa Barbara is a mecca for orchid enthusiasts.

Locally farmed flowers typically find their way to the downtown Los Angeles flower district—the largest wholesale flower market in the country. Japanese flower farmers started the market in 1913 after seeing the success of garden entrepreneurs such as Ventura County's Theodosia Shepherd (1845–1906), who pioneered the nation's cut-flower industry when she began selling her backyard bounty in the late 1800s. *See also California Poppy.*

Food trucks of all flavors congregate for a weekly gathering in the Highland Park neighborhood of Los Angeles, CA

FOOD TRUCK

The estimated 7,000 food trucks that crawl through Los Angeles are descendants of the city's **tamale** cart craze of the late 1800s, and are in part responsible for the national food truck trend of the late 2000s. By the 1970s Los Angeles had the country's largest concentration of Mexican immigrants, who largely popularized *loncheras*— stationary food trucks serving affordable fast food. Many vendors simply carted cooked foods around, until one operator equipped his truck with a stove in 1974, making them true roving kitchens. Los Angeles County started licensing the trucks in the 1980s and applying health standards similar to those for restaurants. Despite their "roach coach" moniker, the trucks must drive to a sanitized commissary nightly to be cleaned and restocked before returning to work each day.

Many loncheras are family-run landmarks in their neighborhoods, some so famous that people travel great distances for a taco, *ceviche*, or *mulita* (sandwich-style taco). Traditional trucks still thrive, even as the hunger for gourmet fusion trucks was ignited by chef Roy Choi (1970–), who introduced his Kogi truck in 2008. Choi's genius wasn't just his sensational mix of Korean and Mexican recipes, but the use of Twitter feeds to alert the hungry to the truck's whereabouts. The model caught on, and a food fad was reborn. Now diners can scout for *dhosas*, lobster grilled cheese, and *bánh mi* sandwiches as they combat traffic, chasing the trucks that hope to be the next big thing. *See also Burrito, Taco, and Tamale.*

Interstate 110 (Harbor Freeway) and Interstate 105 (Century Freeway) meet in Los Angeles, CA •
Courtesy of Google Earth

FREEWAY

Southern California is the birthplace of car culture, where car customization emerged and carcentric amenities such as motels, drive-thrus, drive-ins, **strip malls**, **valet parking**, and self-service gas stations have thrived. Los Angeles County has led the nation in per-capita automobile ownership since 1915, enabling Los Angeles—a metropolis with a distinct downtown core—to become "72 suburbs in search of a city," as author Dorothy Parker (1893–1967) once quipped. These separate districts were eventually united by "motor parkways," the first of which linked downtown Los Angeles and Pasadena in 1939. The landscape is now dominated by an interlinked system of roadways, and traveling on them is a California ritual. To drive a freeway became "a special way of being alive," wrote architecture critic Reyner Banham (1922–1988) in 1971, "a state of heightened awareness that some locals find mystical."

Residents use a local parlance of freeway numbers to refer to specific routes. The 50-mile jaunt from Burbank to Costa Mesa might sound something like, "Take the 5 to the 605 to the 405 to the 55." Life on the road is also tied to two local tools: the Thomas Guide, a pre-GPS-era book of detailed street maps, and SigAlert.com, an up-to-the-minute Web site that shows freeway congestion. *See also Custom Car, Fast-Food Burger, Programmatic Architecture, Shopping Mall, Smog, and Strip Mall.*

A berry-covered serving of Pinkberry's classic yogurt at a store in Westlake Village, CA

FROZEN YOGURT

When frozen yogurt hit it big in the 1980s and 1990s, its typically tangy taste was masked with sugar and it was billed as a low-fat alternative to ice cream. But in 2005 fro-yo was remastered and reintroduced by Pinkberry, a tiny shop in West Hollywood. By tweaking the sugar content, Pinkberry unleashed yogurt's innate tartness and offered a plethora of toppings for its two original flavors—plain and green tea. While the so-called "Crackberry" addicts might tout the taste, a major component of the chain's megapopularity is the sleek appearance of its stores, which have become hip gathering places for design-minded youth.

Snowberry, IceBerry, Menchie's, and Kiwiberri are just a few of the imitators born of the Pinkberry craze. To stay competitive in the highly saturated frozen yogurt market, retailers like YogurtLand have introduced pay-by-weight pricing, while others have gone for pure gimmickry, offering wacky flavors or extra-flashy environments.

Although each chain attempts to differentiate itself, many fro-yo retailers have the commonality of Korean American ownership, which may not be a coincidence. Korea-based Red Mango, which opened in Seoul in 2002, is the likely inspiration for this new generation of frozen dessert that is healthy, tart, offered in limited flavors, and dished up in highly styled settings.

A fruit cart vendor slices and dices fruit near Venice Beach in Los Angeles, CA

FRUIT CART

Of all the street food options in Los Angeles, there isn't a better deal or healthier option than at a fruit cart. With their telltale rainbow-emblazoned umbrellas protecting both the fruit and vendors from the heat of the sun, these mobile fruit stands aren't hard to find either. Vendors typically set up shop on busy intersections, in front of bus stops, or in neighborhood sidewalks with heavy pedestrian traffic.

An array of peeled fruits are carefully arranged on ice at the top of the glass enclosed carts, ready to be picked and sliced. Around $6 will buy a large bag of fruits; $4 will buy a small size. Customers pick from pineapple, mango, cantaloupe, watermelon, coconut, jicama, cucumber, and papaya, or they can opt for the whole mix. The fruits are sliced to order, placed into a bag, doused with freshly squeezed lime juice, sprinkled with salted chile powder, and topped with a plastic fork—the same way that fresh fruit is often taken in Mexico. The result makes for a refreshing snack at just about any time of day. *See also Food Truck and Hot Dog.*

Workers scurry to serve hungry brunch-goers at Pann's Restaurant & Coffee Shop (1958) in Los Angeles, CA

GOOGIE STYLE

California welcomed the Space Age of the 1950s and 1960s with enthusiasm and style, seen in everything from rocketlike automobiles to home furnishings blanketed with atomic motifs. But architecture most fully expressed the era's technological advances, sense of optimism, and preoccupation with space travel. From these societal developments evolved Googie architecture—an exaggerated, modern style that defined the 1950s coffee shop and was also used in bowling alleys, motels, and gas stations. The term *Googie* comes from an innovative 1949 design by John Lautner (1911–1994) for Googie's restaurant, which stood on the Sunset Strip until it was demolished in 1989. The building featured expansive glass windows, a gravity-defying roof, sharp angles, overreaching canopies, exposed steel beams, an open kitchen, and bold signage oriented to street traffic. Architects eagerly imitated the look, including the prolific office of Armét & Davis (considered the Frank Lloyd Wright of 1950s coffee shops), whose projects include Pann's, Johnie's, and several Norms restaurants.

Although the style never gained critical acceptance, its commercial success made business owners happy to leave a trail of Tomorrowlands. Many examples of this quirky genre have succumbed to bulldozers, but Googie icons such as Hollywood's Cinerama Dome theater, the LAX Theme Building, and countless Denny's restaurants survive as the real-life architecture of the Jetsons. *See also Midcentury Modern Design and Modern Architecture.*

Paste-ups, stickers, tags, stencils, and graffiti cover the side of a building in downtown Los Angeles, CA

GRAFFITI

Like many urban centers worldwide, Greater Los Angeles is a major destination for graffiti writers, where "bombers" endeavor to plaster their names wherever they can. Based almost purely on letterforms, graffiti ranges from simple tags done with markers or spray cans to elaborate, multicolored pieces—often the collaborative effort of an associated crew. Although controversial, this youthful expression of identity is clearly a product of love. Writers must contend with law enforcement, gang violence, and buffers—such as Los Angeles's Graffiti Guerrilla—to get their work seen, and it may only last a few hours.

While Southern California's graffiti evolved from the East Coast hip-hop culture of the 1970s, it has been heavily influenced by *placas*, a 1930s tradition of territory marking by Latinos in Los Angeles. Other Latino themes, such as Old English black lettering and the use of *calaveras* (skulls)—popularized by the influential veteran writer Chaz Bojorquez (1949–)—differentiates L.A.'s style. Another defining feature is local **surf** and **skateboard** culture reflected in **beach** city graffiti.

Among favored graffiti spots, including **billboards**, cement riverbeds, and **freeway** overpasses, none can replace the Belmont Tunnel in Los Angeles as a mecca for graffiti art. The tunnel was once a downtown thruway for the historic Pacific Electric Railway, but its entrance was sealed in 2008 to accommodate an adjacent apartment complex.

Mating grunions mass on Cabrillo Beach in San Pedro, CA • Courtesy of the Cabrillo Marine Aquarium

GRUNION

Between March and August, two to six nights after a full or new moon, crowds gather on sandy **beaches** from Baja California to Santa Barbara and wait. This may sound like a group of occultists about to take part in a mystical ritual, but they await another ritual of sorts—the complex mating of small, silvery fish known as grunions (*Leuresthes tenuis*). During mating season, and only on nights when the tides are highest, thousands of grunions beach themselves for a minute or two to lay a few hundred eggs each. Females ride a wave to the shore, dig their bodies into the sand, and deposit their eggs, while the males gather around and release milt, which fertilizes the eggs.

While most humans simply take in the fanciful sight of shoals of fish dancing on the shores in the moonlight, others come to fish. Fishing is only allowed with bare hands, and individuals aged 16 and over must also have a California fishing license. Specially trained observers called Grunion Greeters also participate in grunion runs. These volunteers capture data about each spawning so that scientists can continue to explore the lives of these fascinating creatures.

A man shows off his muscles at Muscle Beach Gym on the Venice Beach Boardwalk in Los Angeles, CA

HEALTH AND FITNESS

Southern California is the epicenter of American physical fitness, where the quest for the perfect body, an outdoor lifestyle, and an openness to new ideas allows trends such as hula hooping, inline skating, Jazzercise, and boot camps to thrive. The Golden State has a history of health and fitness fanaticism, but the interest in one's own physique flourished as an integral element of Southern California's **beach** culture, where suntanned bodies are always on display.

The original Muscle Beach, off the Santa Monica **Pier**, was the locus of athleticism in the 1930s, 1940s, and 1950s. Crowds gathered there to watch gravity-defying acrobatics, gymnastic performances, power lifters, and hard bodies. In 1959 the site was closed, and activity resumed at its current location, on the Venice Beach Boardwalk. As meccas of physical fitness, these venues have seen the rise of megamuscleman Steve "Hercules" Reeves (1926–2000), fitness evangelist Jack LaLanne (1914–2011), early gym owner Joe Gold (1922–2004), bodybuilding pioneer Joe Weider (1919–2013), and former California Governor Arnold Schwarzenegger (1947–).

Body image and physical health are still of singular importance in the region, where gyms, yoga studios, vegetarian eateries, and health **spas** are all a part of the culture, and the newest health trends are sure to find an audience. *See also Spa.*

Mirrors, bold color, classicism, modernism, and a touch of glamour greet guests at the Viceroy Santa Monica Hotel in Santa Monica, CA • Courtesy of Viceroy Santa Monica

HOLLYWOOD REGENCY STYLE

Fashion has long expressed the glamour of old Hollywood. In the 1940s interiors became another canvas to showcase this lavish world in a style known as Hollywood Regency—an eclectic mix of neoclassical, Art Deco, Chippendale, and **modern** furnishings. Mirrored tiles, grandiose moldings, splashy prints, oversize furniture, bold colors, chinoiserie, and funky objets d'art provide enough drama to match the vibrant lifestyles of Tinseltown's glitterati.

Dorothy Draper (1889–1969)—interior decorating's trailblazer—is credited with the creation of Hollywood Regency, first seen at the Arrowhead Springs Hotel and **Spa** in 1939. The homes of movie stars were soon filled with the style's signature look, and other designers, such as William Haines (1900–1973) and Billy Baldwin (1903–1984), got in on the fun.

Draper's assertion that "the Drab Age is over" rings true with each revival that Hollywood Regency enjoys. The style was updated in the 1960s as a counterpoint to the minimalism of the Modern movement. Its current popularity, fueled by the work of Kelly Wearstler (1967–) and Jonathan Adler (1966–), provides a counterpoint to the grim asceticism of the 1990s loft look. Today hip hotels such as the Parker Palms in Palm Springs and the Viceroy chain are among the best spots to view this ever-evolving and unmistakable style.

A hot dog vender makes a sale in downtown Los Angeles, CA

HOT DOG

Don't tell this to Chicagoans or New Yorkers, but residents of Los Angeles eat more hot dogs than people do in any other city in the country. This isn't hard to believe when you drive down La Brea Avenue and see the line for Pink's hot dog stand well before you turn into the parking lot. As much a part of the Los Angeles experience as the Hollywood sign, Pink's has been serving up its famous chili dogs since 1939. An entire decade prior, Los Angeles made hot dog history when the words became the first ever to be uttered in a cartoon by Mickey Mouse in *The Karnival Kid* (1929).

A few miles east, in downtown Los Angeles, Latino street vendors wrap their dogs in bacon, reviving a Mexican tradition that some consider the city's official hot dog style. By grilling the meat—and not steaming or boiling it (as county health code requires)—vendors risk fines and jail time, which hasn't stopped the selling of, or the demand for, this gastronomic indulgence.

Another local legend is the Southland's Oki dog—two wieners slathered with chili, cheese, and **pastrami**, then wrapped in an oversize **burrito** tortilla. This heart attack guarantee, which at one time fueled Los Angeles's early punk scene, can be experienced at Oki's Dog on Pico Boulevard or Oki Dog on Fairfax Avenue.

A jacaranda-lined street awash in purple blooms in Santa Barbara, CA

JACARANDA

JAK-uh-RAN-duh For much of the time, jacarandas are like many other trees in Southern California—unrecognizable amid the urban greenscape. But twice a year jacarandas suddenly blossom en masse into a vibrant violet, which earns them the notice they deserve. The fragrant, trumpet-shaped flowers bloom most intensely in late spring, and then again from November to December. Especially impressive are jacaranda-lined streets, which create breathtaking corridors of purple in places like Ash Street in San Diego, Palm Drive in Beverly Hills, and Del Mar Boulevard in Pasadena (the city is home to 3,500 jacarandas). Despite these beautiful displays, the trees are best loved in a neighbor's yard, where the flowers can shed and leave their infamous sticky residue for someone else to clean up.

The renowned horticulturalist Kate Sessions (1857–1940) introduced jacarandas to Southern California when she planted imported seeds throughout San Diego and its beloved Balboa Park. Blue jacaranda (*Jacaranda mimosifolia*) is the region's most common species, and it flourishes in dry, sunny weather. Native to the arid plains of Argentina and Brazil, jacarandas are also associated with Pretoria, South Africa; Australia's Queensland; and Buenos Aires, Argentina; all of which share Southern California's temperate climate.

Two lonely jackrabbit homesteads at dusk in Wonder Valley, CA

JACKRABBIT HOMESTEAD

Artists, outdoor enthusiasts, and those harried by city life have been drawn to Southern California's high desert for recreation, inspiration, and meditation for more than a century. In 1938 the federal government helped to formalize the process of desert living by enacting the Small Tract Act, which allowed for private ownership of publicly owned scrubland. For a nominal fee, homesteaders willing to live without electricity, roads, or access to water were given deeds for up to five acres. Participation in the program surged after World War II, when advances such as air conditioning eased the harsh realities of desert life. These "jackrabbit homesteads," some with names such as Calloused Palms, Canta-Forda Rancho, and Withering Heights, were mostly owned by working-class Angelenos.

Although some cabins have been enjoyed over several generations, the legacy of the program is an estimated 2,500 shanties scattered throughout the Morongo basin that, for the most part, now house only weeds and desert critters. Some area residents cheered when a 1999 program called Shack Attack razed more than 100 derelict structures, while others decried the measure, citing the cabins as historic landmarks. Recently, they have been given a new life as creative spaces for artists, who find particular charm in their weather-beaten, *wabi-sabi* qualities.

The sun sets behind a cluster of Joshua trees in Joshua Tree National Park • Paul Richter

JOSHUA TREE

Resembling a cross between a spiky yucca plant and a branchy tree, Joshua trees (*Yucca brevifolia*) have a look all their own, making them icons of the Mojave Desert. The Mojave occupies the high desert areas of California's Joshua Tree National Park, with elevations between 1,300 and 5,900 feet. This unique habitat is higher, wetter, and somewhat cooler than the adjacent Colorado Desert, and the only place in the world where Joshua trees grow.

The upward-facing limbs of this tall, thorny shrub reminded Mormons traversing the Mojave Desert in the mid-19th century of Joshua, the biblical prophet who led the Israelites into the Promised Land. Once thought to be members of the lily family (*Liliaceae*) due to their creamy white springtime blossoms, Joshua trees are now classified as monocotyledon (monocot) trees, making them relatives of grasses and orchids.

Although the early California Senator John C. Frémont (1813–1890) considered them to be "the most repulsive trees in the vegetable kingdom," plenty of desert inhabitants have found great use for the plants. Joshua trees have provided food and fiber for Native Americans, fencing material for homesteaders, and fuel for miners, not to mention picture-perfect silhouettes for dazzling desert sunsets. Birds also love the trees. Of the 78 bird species known to nest in Joshua Tree National Park, 25 of them choose Joshua trees as their perch of choice.

Beach-goers frolic at Salt Creek Beach on a hot July day in Dana Point, CA

LIFEGUARD TOWER

Beyond *Baywatch*, the lifeguard tower is an icon of Southern California's coastline. Originally all-wooden structures, these towers give some of the world's most distinguished lifeguards a higher perspective to scan for endangered swimmers and dangerous ocean conditions. Today the structures are made of wood and fiberglass and are numbered according to their district, allowing for easy identification and navigation. Tide boards on the back of each tower denote current tide schedules, water temperature, and conditions. Flags indicate any hazards or no-**surfing** zones (areas designated for swimmers and bodyboarders only).

Although lifeguards have been employed since the 1930s, the highly competitive occupation did not become official until 1951, when Huntington **Beach** organized a state lifeguard program. Now some 700 lifeguards make more than 10,000 rescues each year on state beaches.

The hundreds of towers that line SoCal's shores have inevitably influenced local architecture. In Hermosa Beach, two contemporary homes embody this littoral typology. Perhaps the most celebrated tower mimicry is Venice Beach's Norton House (1983), designed by architect Frank Gehry (1929–). The home was built with its own lifeguard tower gazing out to sea. *See also Beach.*

A classic "bird bath" margarita at Casa Guadalajara restaurant in Old Town San Diego, CA

MARGARITA

Tequila, lime juice, and Cointreau (or triple sec) make up America's most ordered drink—the margarita. The origin of this refreshing cocktail is hazy, and creation myths abound. Dallas socialite Margarita Sames (1911–2009) claimed she developed the drink at her Acapulco villa in 1948. Several other bartenders have alleged that they named the concoction for specific Hollywood actresses they regularly served, such as Rita Hayworth (1918–1987), who has a Margarita namesake. While Hollywood circles certainly helped to popularize the drink, it is more likely that today's margarita developed from the similarly mixed Tequila Daisy drink.

Margarita, after all, is the Spanish word for daisy.

Margaritas were originally served shaken, on the rocks, with a wedge of lime and salt on the rim. When the automated soft-serve machine was introduced in 1971, the cocktail was recast as the ultimate frozen party refreshment, colored and flavored with a variety of fruits.

Margaritas are as easy to find in Southern California as jazz is in New Orleans. Of the many worthy establishments, El Cholo is beloved by locals; it has been serving the drink since 1967. The demand for the El Cholo margaritas has made the chain the world's largest buyer of 1800 Tequila.

Two men saunter by a mural of marijuana activist Jack Herer by Brian "TAZROC" Garcia (2013), which marks the Nile Collective in the Venice Beach neighborhood of Los Angeles, CA

MARIJUANA DISPENSARY

A topic of endless civic and political debate, marijuana dispensaries, or cannabis collectives, are easy to spot throughout Southern California. With green crosses that serve as beacons, dispensaries offer legal, medical-grade marijuana alongside cannabis-based treats ranging from brownies and lollipops to butter and cooking oil.

In 1996 California passed the Compassionate Use Act, which allows the use of cannabis with a doctor's recommendation. In 2003 the aptly titled Senate Bill 420, the Medical Marijuana Program Act, started a voluntary identification system in which patients receive ID cards from county health departments to confirm their medical marijuana status. Since then over 80,000 cards have been issued, and the number of dispensaries has grown exponentially. Cities have responded with moratoriums on new establishments, as well as restrictions on where the storefronts can be placed in relation to schools and parks. While the Obama administration declared in 2009 that it would not raid collectives, the tension between state and national jurisdictions has put the dispensaries in limbo, with raids and store closings on the uptick.

Denoting both questionable alley operations and open-door shops, the green cross is still a common sight across Southern California. Just ask any pedestrian on Venice Beach's famed boardwalk, where scrubs-clad promoters tout "The Doctor Is In" and waiting rooms are usually filled.

Evangelicals gather on a Sunday morning at the Crystal Cathedral (1981) in Garden Grove, CA prior to its sale to the Roman Catholic Diocese of Orange and name change to the Christ Cathedral

MEGACHURCH

In the suburbs between Los Angeles and San Diego is an area known as Southern California's Bible Belt. There the faithful gather to worship in stadium-size congregations, complete with jumbotrons, Christian rock music, and concert lighting. Megachurches have at least 2,000 congregants and are a growing national phenomenon. Individuals disillusioned with traditional religion find their faith reenergized by charismatic ministers, upbeat messages, and nondenominational services offered seven days a week, often tailored to special interest groups such as dog lovers or outdoor enthusiasts.

California leads the charge in this religious movement, with nearly 200 megachurches across the state. Almost a century in the making, jumbo congregations grew out of the innovations of several pioneering and media-savvy church leaders in Southern California. In the 1920s and 1930s the fiery Aimee Semple McPherson (1890–1944) utilized radio, high drama, and theatrical antics to draw thousands of followers to her Angelus Temple in Echo Park—perhaps the first megachurch in America. Another enterprising minister, the Reverend Robert H. Schuller (1926–2015), appealed to the newly car-centric lifestyles of Orange County by preaching to carloads of parishioners at his drive-in church in Garden Grove in the 1950s. The massive Crystal Cathedral was later built on the site and became the home for Schuller's *Hour of Power* television ministry.

The Millard Sheets-designed Chase Bank (1970, formerly a Home Savings bank) on Sunset Boulevard features motion picture themed mosaics in the Hollywood district of Los Angeles, CA

MIDCENTURY BANK

Featuring **modern design** and impressive works of art, Southern California's midcentury banks are testaments to the region's concentrated wealth and culture of commerce. By the 1950s an expanding car culture prompted banks to open newly conceived "branches" in suburban neighborhoods where convenience, exceptional customer service, and memorable architecture gave them a competitive edge.

Palm Springs is one of the best places to see architecturally significant banks, notably the original City National Bank. Now a Bank of America, this "cathedral of commerce," as the architect called it, draws attention with its upturned white roof and blue-tiled, curving walls. Victor Gruen and Associates (of **shopping mall** fame) designed the building in 1959 as a nod to the Cha-

pel of Notre Dame du Haut (1955) by Le Corbusier (1887–1965). Other local modernists, such as E. Stewart Williams (1909–2005), also produced noteworthy banks in Palm Springs.

Equally impressive but decidedly different are the travertine-clad and gold-trimmed works of Millard Sheets (1907–1989). His designs are immediately recognizable for their stripped-down classicism, magnificent mosaics, and stained-glass **murals** that depict themes from California's history. Although Sheets had no formal architectural training, Howard F. Ahmanson Sr. (1906–1968) entrusted the celebrated artist with the design of more than 50 Home Savings and Loan branches (now Chase) scattered throughout the Los Angeles basin. *See also Modern Architecture.*

A Ray and Charles Eames-designed desk, storage unit, and molded plastic chair • Courtesy of Herman Miller, Inc.

MIDCENTURY MODERN DESIGN

The 1930s through the mid-1960s was an unprecedented era of innovation in architectural, interior, and industrial design in California. The confluence of newly developed wartime materials and technologies, and a local culture of exuberant experimentation led to a wealth of goods that shaped the lives of average Americans. Surfboard, furniture, and automobile production, for example, was reinvigorated by the use of fiberglass—a material fine-tuned for aviation projects during World War II.

While California's influence in this realm began in the 1930s, with help from forward-thinking European émigrés, it was the postwar years when the state's **Modern** movement blossomed. A fresh aesthetic in textiles, furnishings, fashion, and tableware inspired a new mode of living that obscured the lines between indoors and outdoors. Shelter magazines such as *Better Homes and Gardens* helped to spread the gospel of SoCal's stubborn sunshine and informality, with aspirational spreads devoted to light-filled homes and California-designed wares. Simplicity, organic forms, and accessibility are the hallmarks of this movement.

The office of Charles and Ray Eames (1907–1978 and 1912–1988) embodied the spirit of Southern California's innumerable pioneers of Modernist design. In their aim to reach the most people with the best design at the lowest cost, the iconic couple left behind an impressive legacy still beloved today. *See also Googie Style and Modern Architecture.*

The belltower and lush gardens of Mission San Juan Capistrano's inner courtyard in San Juan Capistrano, CA

MISSION

In 1769 a Franciscan friar named Junipero Serra (1713–1784) led an expedition from Mexico into the area now known as San Diego to begin construction of the first mission in Alta (Upper) California. As part of an effort by the Spanish government to colonize the territory and convert its original inhabitants to Christianity, the mission chain was expanded to 21 outposts by 1823. Mission complexes were placed approximately one day's journey along El Camino Real (the King's Road), linking San Diego in the south to Sonoma in the north.

Missionaries introduced numerous products, ideas, traditions, and styles that are still reflected in California lives and landscapes. Not all were positive influences, however. By the mid-1800s foreign diseases had killed off nearly two-thirds of the state's Native American population. These communities, who largely provided the muscle to build the mission complexes, also endured enforced slavery, alienation, and land loss as a result of the imposed system.

In 1830, after Mexico won independence from Spain, the missions were secularized and handed over to private owners. This conversion subjected the fragile structures to further decline until the 1884 publication of *Ramona*, a romance novel by Helen Hunt Jackson (1830–1885), inspired a movement of mission preservation and restoration. Today more than 5.5 million tourists visit California's missions each year, making these monuments the state's most visited historic attractions. *See also Mission Revival Style.*

Crowds gather for a festival on the grounds of the Bowers Museum (1931) in Santa Ana, CA

MISSION REVIVAL STYLE

In the late 1880s an architectural movement called **Mission** Revival emerged in California, inspired by the missions of the state's earliest Spanish settlers. The style's simple stucco forms and spare use of decorative iron and wood helped ignite America's romance with its own exotic Far West. The materials and construction were well suited to Southern California's Mediterranean climate, making Mission Revival an authentic regional alternative to imported East Coast architecture. When western railroad companies adopted Mission Revival style for station depots and hotels, its characteristic arched walkways, stuccoed walls, low-pitched and red-tiled roofs, parapets, bell towers, and quatrefoil windows were a hit. Its popularity spread eastward, prompting the reversal of America's previous architectural migrations.

Enthusiasm for this instantly recognizable style peaked between the 1890s and 1915, when it was used profusely for post offices, schools, churches, libraries, resorts, and residences. After World War I tastes began to shift toward the more sophisticated European and **Spanish Colonial Revival styles**, but throughout the 20th century, and especially today, the look of Mission Revival architecture forms the basis for Southern California's visual identity. Its key elements are still incorporated into contemporary buildings, from **strip malls** to gas stations, reinforcing the romantic image of the region's simpler, pastoral days. *See also Mission and Spanish Colonial Revival Style.*

The William F. Cody-designed Jaffe House (1963) in Rancho Mirage, CA • Sean Garrison of Shooting LA

MODERN ARCHITECTURE

Modern architecture in Southern California is not as much an aesthetic as it is a way of life. When new possibilities in construction emerged after World War II, the modern idea of living in open, flowing spaces with little distinction between indoors and out could be fully realized. While these notions had their beginnings in the gray climate of Bauhaus Germany, they flourished in Southern California amid an informal culture under perpetually sunny skies.

In the early 20th century early Modernists such as Irving Gill (1870–1936) and Richard Neutra (1892–1870) introduced International style attributes—flat roofs, open floor plans, walls of glass, and minimal ornamentation. Later architects, including John Lautner (1911–1994),

put their own spin on modern ideas in buildings throughout the Los Angeles basin, as did the likes of Albert Frey (1903–1998) in Palm Springs, where a slightly different approach called Desert Modernism took root.

Modernism manifested itself in myriad ways, from see-through homes to futuristic **Googie** coffee shops to panoramic supermarkets—all with a common thread of openness and the creation of unity between shelter and nature. After 1945 Modernism went beyond the realms of commercial buildings, custom residences, and **Case Study** concept homes when developers such as Joseph Eichler (1900–1974) introduced Modern housing to the masses in suburban tract homes. *See also Case Study House, Googie Style, and Midcentury Modern Design.*

Climbers set up a slackline between North and South Horror Rocks in the Hall of Horrors area of Joshua Tree National Park

MONZOGRANITE

Huge piles of boulders, sometimes in surprisingly geometric formations, typify the rocky, sculptural landscape of **Joshua Tree** National Park. A type of rock known as monzogranite underlies much of the park—and Southern California's vast mountain ranges in general—and it is the medium by which weathering and erosion have created scores of fantastic landforms. Local monzogranite was created more than 100 million years ago when magma in the planet's crust oozed toward the surface. A slow cooling process allowed large, tightly locked crystals to form with a fabric of perfectly horizontal and vertical jointing. Erosion by wind and water gradually unearthed these blocks of rock and loosened pressure along the joints, leaving boxy boulders scattered in massive pilings.

Some of the distinctive contours of Southern California's mountainous and desert landscapes follow geologic typologies. Isolated bedrock knobs and small mountains amid an otherwise level plain are *inselbergs* (German for "island mountain"). A large, high rock or piling, often found atop an inselberg, is called a *tor*. The more surreal-looking *hoodoos* are molded when softer material erodes beneath a harder top rock, leaving mushroom-shaped or precariously balanced rocks. These and other features have resulted in a multitude of climbing and bouldering opportunities in Joshua Tree National Park, which boasts 400 official climbing formations and 8,000 climbing routes. *See also Joshua Tree.*

The State Theater (1921) in downtown Los Angeles, CA • Berger/Conser Photography from the book "The Last Remaining Seats"

MOVIE PALACE

There was a time in the history of moviegoing when theaters were made to usher audiences out of reality and into elaborate fantasy worlds. Movie places were enchanting retreats, complete with glittering chandeliers, sweeping staircases, coiffed ceilings, ornately painted plasterwork, and powder rooms to suit the most fastidious customers. With spectacular facades that channeled everything from Mayan temples to Spanish Renaissance castles, movie palaces elevated the act of watching a movie or show to an art form. As theater owner Marcus Loew (1870–1927) once said, "We sell tickets to theaters, not movies."

These entertainment temples sprang up in cities across America after Sid Grauman (1879–1950) built his Million Dollar Theater in Los Angeles in 1918. Some of the most glamorous were found in the city's downtown Broadway theater district, where 12 theaters offered seating for 17,000 people, fulfilling the voracious appetite for "pictures" during the Great Depression. Major movie **studios** often operated their own theaters until the practice was deemed monopolistic in 1948.

Today these architectural Norma Desmonds are in various states of disrepair, with some functioning as churches, swap meets, jewelry marts, or nightclubs. For the curious, the Los Angeles Conservancy's Last Remaining Seats film series offers audiences a rare glimpse inside these historic gems. *See also Studio Lot.*

"The Pope of Broadway" mural (1985), a tribute to actor Anthony Quinn, by Eloy Torrez in downtown Los Angeles, CA

MURAL

With more murals within its vicinity than any other urban center, Los Angeles has proclaimed itself the mural capital of the world. **Freeway** abutments, walls, and building facades are the canvases for the city's 1,500 public masterpieces. The largest of these, running a half mile along the San Fernando Valley's Tujunga Wash, is *The Great Wall of Los Angeles* by Judy Baca (1946–). It depicts the history of California from the perspective of working-class minorities and exemplifies the city's cultural tradition of the medium, known for messages of social protest, local history, and Chicano heritage.

The modern era of regional mural making began in 1932 when the Work Projects Administration (WPA) commissioned artists to beautify more than 200 public buildings, setting a precedent for government-sponsored art in Los Angeles. This early work, specifically that of José Clemente Orozco (1883–1949), Diego Rivera (1886–1957), and David Alfaro Siqueiros (1896–1974)—three Mexican muralists invited to the city as guests—inspired a new wave of mural making in the 1960s and 1970s.

Due to their exposure, murals require protection. Venice **Beach**'s Social and Public Art Resource Center (SPARC) was founded in 1976 to support mural artists and promote, protect, and conserve existing murals. In 1994 a similar organization was established to create "An Oasis of Murals" in the desert town of Twentynine Palms. *See also Product Mural.*

Dan Koeppel, founder of the Los Angeles Big Parade, takes part in an art event celebrating neighbor-hood stairways in the Highland Park neighborhood of Los Angeles, CA

NEIGHBORHOOD STAIRWAY

Los Angeles is known for its shortage of pedestrians. It also offers something special that only a handful of other urban areas have—miles and miles of hidden staircases that are a siren song for those on their feet.

Originally designed to provide easy access to public transportation, the shortcuts were used by residents to reach their bus or streetcar stops. This infrastructure highlights the widespread ridership of the region's once spectacular public transportation system.

Nearly 300 neighborhood stairways exist between Santa Monica and Pasadena, especially concentrated in the hillside neighborhoods built in the 1920s, such as El Sereno, Highland Park, Mount Washington, Silver Lake, and Echo Park. The Silver Lake neighborhood alone has about 60 stair streets, including Laurel and Hardy's *The Music Box* steps, where the duo attempted to push up a piano in their 1932 short film.

Charles Fleming (1955–), author of *Secret Stairs: A Walking Guide to the Historic Staircases of Los Angeles*, is one of several urban pioneers who has renewed public interest in these little-known gems. His itineraries include neighborhood lore and views of unique backyard hideaways and grand city vistas. Another stair enthusiast, Dan Koeppel, founded Big Parade Los Angeles, a two-day walking event that includes 100 public stairways across 40 miles, from downtown to the Hollywood sign.

A cool winter morning at the Self-Realization Fellowship Lake Shrine Temple in Pacific Palisades, CA

NEW AGE SPIRITUALITY

Whether your chakras need realignment, your soul seeks violet vibrations, or your body craves a spiritual channeling, there's no place better to do it than Southern California. The region's smorgasbord of spirituality makes it one of the most diverse religious communities in the world, with New Age philosophies well represented. The multitude of meditation centers, psychic's offices, New Age institutes, and incense-burning boutiques attest to the mysticism endemic to the far reaches of the West.

Since the mid-1800s California has been promoted as a place to transform the body, cleanse the soul, and start anew, attracting "cults of cosmic fluidists, astral planers, Emmanuel movers, Rosicrucians and other boozy transcendentalists," as writer Willard Huntington Wright (1888-1939) described the Los Angeles scene in 1913. A steady procession of gurus, swamis, and other enlightened leaders came to Southern California and established spiritual communities such as the Theosophical and Vedanta Societies, Self-Realization Fellowship, and Meditation Mount, all of which remain active today.

Celebrities have been instrumental in the mainstream acceptance (and mockery) of New Age spirituality. The most well known may be Shirley MacLaine (1934–), who uncovered a new spiritual terrain for Americans with her best-selling book, *Out on a Limb* (1983). One of her muses was the long-running (now defunct) source for all things metaphysical—West Hollywood's Bodhi Tree Bookstore.

Live Oak Park prior to an afternoon of birthday parties in Fallbrook, CA

OAK

Of the many iconic California scenes in which oak trees star, none is as stunning as their dark green silhouettes against golden rolling hills. Oaks are a dominant feature in a wide range of habitats. Whether amid redwoods in the north or cactuses in the south, they appear across more than 11 million acres of California countryside. As a testament to their prevalence, the word oak—including the Spanish equivalents, *robles* (deciduous oak) and *encino* (live oak)—is alluded to in more than 150 place names within the state, not to mention a multitude of streets, schools, and parks.

The first Spanish explorers named these abundant trees after Spain's own shrub oak, *chaparra*, and **chaparral** (the place of scrub oaks) was soon used to denote the native grassland where the trees thrived. The trees provide habitat for hundreds of species of wildlife and help to protect in-ground water supplies. Fall acorns are forage for many animals and once were a staple food for Native Americans.

All California oaks belong to the genus *Quercus*, with the scrub oak (*Quercus dumosa*) and coast live oak (*Quercus agrifolia*) the most common. Scrub oaks are typically fewer than 12 feet tall, with several trunks emerging from the ground, while evergreen coast live oaks have a single trunk and can grow more than 75 feet high. *See also Chaparral.*

Ocotillo plants in bloom after a winter rainstorm in Anza-Borrego Desert State Park, CA

OCOTILLO

With tall, spindly arms reaching up to the sky, the ocotillo (*Fouquieria splendens*) is an unexpected bit of visual whimsy among the plant life of the Sonoran and Chihuahuan Deserts. This is especially the case during times of rain, when the shrub's leggy branches sprout small green leaves along its normally dry and prickly branches. From March to June the branch tips burst with vibrant crimson blooms. The sweet nectar attracts both hummingbirds and bees, which pollinate the flowers. The fruit contains winged seeds that fly on the wind. Both the fruit and flowers once provided sustenance, as well as medicine, for the indigenous Cahuilla people.

Ocotillo shrubs can reach about 20 feet tall, and without a true trunk to hold the branches, can look like a bundle of sticks arising from an underground core. This strange appearance has given the ocotillo several different names, including desert coral, Jacob's staff, slimwood, coach whip, and the somewhat misleading vine cactus. Although its sharp spines may suggest otherwise, an ocotillo is not a cactus.

A pumpjack pulls oil from the Long Beach Oil Field beneath a suburban neighborhood in Signal Hill, CA

OIL PUMP

In 1892, just a few decades after California's gold rush, Edward L. Doheny (1856–1935) ignited a frenzy after he struck oil near downtown Los Angeles. Black gold would make countless men wealthy and give new life to a region that was considered to have a worrying lack of accessible energy sources. Southern California's coastal plains were soon covered with dense forests of towering oil derricks, and residents dug up their lawns in hopes of striking it rich, turning neighborhoods into overnight oil shantytowns.

La brea, Spanish for tar, had long been used to waterproof native baskets, canoes, and the adobe roofs of early European settlers, but no one had imagined the vast reservoir of oil that lay underground, even after Doheny's discovery. But when a gusher erupted on Signal Hill in Long **Beach** in 1921, Southern California instantaneously transformed into the "Kuwait of the Jazz Age," according to journalist Eric Schlosser (1959–), and became one of the largest oil producers in the world.

Still a major competitor, California ranks fourth nationwide in volume of pumped oil (although it is the the only oil-producing state that does not tax oil extraction). While new technology has eliminated the majority of the pumping devices that once dominated the landscape, camouflaged derricks stealthily operate amid schools, **shopping malls**, parks, and along the coast. These and pumpjacks (shown) yield an average of 666,000 barrels of oil each day.

A Pacific gray whale shows its fluke (tail) in Southern Californian waters • Courtesy of Cabrillo Marine Aquarium

PACIFIC GRAY WHALE

In winter months the California coast hosts one of the world's longest mammalian migrations. From the chilly Alaskan Arctic down to Mexico's Baja Peninsula lagoons, Pacific gray whales (*Eschrichtius robustus*) make a round-trip journey of up to 14,000 miles. In the fall they begin their two- to three-month trip south to Mexico, passing through California's Santa Cruz and Santa Rosa Islands to give birth in warmer waters. The whales return north in the spring, after their calves have had time to thicken their blubber. Careful observers can catch glimpses of the mammals cruising through Santa Barbara Harbor, Point Dume, and Dana Point in April and May.

Gray whales are distinguished by a distinctive, V-shaped blow and long, sleek bodies with mottled gray-and-white patches—the result of barnacle growth and whale lice. Both males and females can weigh up to 40 tons, making them a comparatively small mysticete (baleen whale). Although they seem to be gentle giants, early whalers called gray whale cows "devilfish" during their migration due to their violent behavior when protecting calves.

Endangered since the early 20th century, the gray whale has since regained its 20,000-plus population after the creatures were given protected status in 1947. In 1994 they were the first marine mammals to be removed from the United States Endangered Species List.

Cucumber-chile, canteloupe, coconut, mango, mamey and strawberry paletas are lined up for choosing at Mateo's Ice Cream and Fruit Bars in Los Angeles, CA

PALETA

Nothing says summertime like sweet blocks of ice on a stick. One local variety hails from Mexico's state of Michoacán and is far from your typical American-style popsicle. *Paletas* are based on traditional Mexican recipes that showcase some of the country's best culinary delights. Unlike the juice-only style typically found in the United States, paletas feature large chunks of fresh fruit frozen in their natural juices. Some are milk or cream based, including those made with generous portions of whole nuts. While familiar flavors such as **strawberry** and watermelon are available, it is the comparably exotic varieties that win devotees—*leche quemada* (smoked milk), *pitaya* (cactus fruit), *nance* (yellow cherry), *rompope con*

pasas (eggnog and raisins), *jamaica* (hibiscus), *guanabana* (soursop, or custard apple), *tejocote* (Mexican crab apple), and *mango con chile* (mango peppered with chili powder).

While paletas are much more common in Mexico than they are in California, most grocers and convenience stores in Latino neighborhoods stock them. For the freshest and tastiest kind, head straight to a *paleteria*, where these icy treats are likely to be handmade and available in exotic flavors. Mateo's Ice Cream, with locations in Culver City and Los Angeles, as well as Neveria Tocumbo in San Diego, are great places to include on your journey for these unforgettable frozen treats.

Palm trees at dusk in the Leimert Park neighborhood of Los Angeles, CA

PALM TREE

Southern California may be one of the few densely populated regions of the world with an emblematic skyline of trees. Despite many recognizable man-made buildings, the enduring image of the region is a row of palms against perpetually blue skies. Of the 3,000 or so known species, just one—the California fan palm (*Washingtonia filifera*)—is a native. Most of the familiar palms that line city streets were imported and planted in the 1920s and 1930s, either for decorative landscaping, to herald special events (particularly the 1932 Olympics), or for movie industry props.

In their natural state, palm trees do not shed their dried fronds. They may hang for decades, making scruffy-looking skirts in which desert animals nest and hide. Palms thrive in groves within desert oases and once provided shade, shelter, tools, and fruit for native peoples of the region. Legend has it that the Oasis of Mara, now known as Twentynine Palms, was created when the indigenous Serrano people planted a palm for the birth of every baby boy over the course of a year.

As much as they symbolize the carefree lifestyle of Southern California, the region's palm trees are aging, and most cities do not replace them. Emissions neutralizing canopy trees—such as ginkgoes and coast live **oaks**—which offer durability and affordability, may soon stand in for beloved palms.

The famous #19 pastrami sandwich awaits a bite at Langer's Delicatessen-Restaurant in Los Angeles, CA

PASTRAMI

Pastrami is the ultimate Jewish deli meat. But delis aren't the only places in SoCal that you'll find this tender specialty. Countless burger joints and fast-food restaurants offer it up in everything from traditional deli-style sandwiches to the region's quirky Oki dog. In fact, alongside **burgers** and **hot dogs**, pastrami completes Southern California's unholy trio of fast-food offerings. Venues across the city claim theirs to be famous, and while this isn't always true, the thriving, and some say unrivaled, Jewish deli scene in and around Los Angeles does dish up some of the world's best beef, steamed to perfection.

The making of pastrami—by brining, seasoning, dry curing, smoking, and steaming beef navel or brisket—is a method for preserving meat. The owner of Langer's Deli, in downtown Los Angeles, claims to steam his meat for up to three hours for an extra measure of tenderness in the legendary #19 sandwich—a near-perfect creation of pastrami, Swiss cheese, Russian dressing, and homemade coleslaw. Elsewhere, classic L.A.–style pastrami is sliced thin, stuffed into a French roll, and served hot and au jus for dipping. The venerable Pasadena-based chain, The Hat, helped to popularize this style, which the restaurant calls the Pastrami Dip. *See also Fast-Food Burger and Hot Dog.*

A male Peninsular bighorn sheep give crowds a view of his horns at the Living Desert Zoo and Gardens in Palm Desert, CA

PENINSULAR BIGHORN SHEEP

Although rarely encountered in the wild, Peninsular bighorn sheep (*Ovis canadensis nelsoni*) are a magnificent sight. Not only do males display impressive coiled horns, the animals are able to maneuver cliffs and rugged terrain with awe-inspiring grace. They use their mountain-climbing skills to quickly escape danger and live in herds to ensure safety in numbers.

For much of the year, males and females commune separately—the ewes, led by a dominant female, take care of their lambs, and the rams roam as bachelors until the fall mating season, when they use their horns in combat for a mate. (The size of the horns, which can weigh up to 30 pounds, indicates a ram's rank within the herd.)

Experts believe bighorn sheep migrated across Siberia to North America via a land bridge 10,000 years ago. This desert subspecies settled in the San Jacinto and Santa Rosa Mountains and south throughout Mexico's Baja Peninsula, but today, this population is endangered. Plagued by disease, encroaching development, drought, and predators (coyotes, mountain lions, and bobcats), herd numbers have plummeted since the arrival of the Spanish in California. Approximately 950 Peninsular bighorn sheep remain in the state, most of which take refuge in Anza-Borrego Desert State Park in San Diego County.

The sun sets beyond the Santa Monica Pier in Santa Monica, CA

PIER

The Southern California coast is home to 20 ocean piers that flow into the sea like fringe on the edge of a rug. Piers are destinations for strolling, dining, shopping, fishing (no license required), riding roller coasters, or simply watching the sun set over the Pacific. Pacific **Beach**'s Crystal Pier even offers visitors the chance to sleep over the ocean in one of its 26 cottages.

Most piers started as cargo terminals, but by the turn of the 20th century they evolved into elaborate, Coney Island–style attractions with fun zones, entertainment venues, arcade games, and amusement rides. The atmosphere of these bygone parks can be experienced at Disney California Adventure Park's Paradise Pier in Anaheim. These pleasure piers were also popular for another reason—they offered easy access to the offshore rumrunner gambling ships during Prohibition.

Unlike Pacific Park in Santa Monica and Belmont Park at **Mission** Beach, both of which still enjoy streams of visitors, most pleasure piers fell into disrepair after World War II. Cultural shifts, storms, fire, and age all took their toll, leaving the once crowded piers to return to the sea. Despite, or perhaps because of, its hazards, the precarious ruins of the one-time Disneyland competitor known as Pacific Ocean Park (POP) were the preferred **surfing** spot for the Z-Boys (of **skateboarding** fame) in the 1970s. *See also Beach, Skateboarding, Surfing, and Theme Park.*

Actors get busy on the set of an adult movie released by Vivid Entertainment • Courtesy of vivid.com

PORNOGRAPHY

Forget Hollywood. The real heart of the entertainment industry is located in a swath of suburbia known as the San Fernando Valley. While Disney, DreamWorks, Universal **Studios**, and Warner Bros. are all based here, mainstream television and movies are only part of the story. The "San Pornando Valley" produces the vast majority of America's X-rated content. Cheap rents, a steady stream of actors seeking work, and close proximity to the movie industry have attracted droves of porn studios to the area since the 1970s (although 2012 legislation requiring condom use has them threatening relocation). To say that pornography has flourished here is a gross understatement—current annual revenue estimates are upward of $13 billion.

Movies such as **Mission** *Asspossible* and *This Ain't Glee XXX* (both 2011) are shot in hidden warehouses, discreet rental properties, and unmarked studios. Illicit filmmaking works much like major Hollywood productions do, save for secrecy, minimal promotional budgets, and lightning speed. It is not uncommon for full-length X-rated films to be filmed, edited, and released in less than a week.

Among the hundreds of adult video producers, Vivid Entertainment is the king of smut, with a record number of Adult Video News (AVN) awards—the Oscars of porn—a cadre of A-list stars, and the credit of inventing the **celebrity** sex tape. The company releases about 60 titles per year. *See also Celebrity and Studio Lot.*

A vintage Singer machine, known as the "invisible repair machine," fixes damaged denim at Schaeffer's Garment Hotel, a full service retail store, denim repair/alteration, and denim manufacturing company in the Hollywood district of Los Angeles, CA

PREMIUM DENIM

Southern California, known for casual attire, isn't just a hot spot for wearing jeans—it's the global center of production, specifically for premium denim. This sector of high-end apparel is labor intensive enough to warrant enormous price tags, from $120 for off the rack to thousands of dollars for custom orders. Through stone washes, resin dips, high-heat drying, sanding, creasing, and final detailing, one pair of jeans might pass through 100 employees and take up to six hours to fabricate. Specialized artisans and renowned denim laundries allow designers such as Adriano Goldschmied (1943–), the "Godfather of Denim," to have their visions made within a few miles of their downtown Los Angeles studios.

While most garment production is done overseas, 85 percent of premium denim is sewn in Los Angeles County, representing $408 million in annual revenue. No one knows for sure how the area became so tangled up in blue, but trendsetting brands such as 7 For All Mankind, Citizens for Humanity, and True Religion probably couldn't exist anywhere else.

Downtown Los Angeles, an important center for the garment trade, has everything needed for the making and selling of apparel. The 100-block fashion district features fabric and accessory wholesalers, sewing facilities, several wholesale apparel showrooms, and Santee Alley, where the bargain-minded seek the latest ghetto chic.

Nachos, milk, Frito pie, chili dogs, Coca-Cola, and dish detergent get equal treatment at the Watts Meat HP Market in the Watts neighborhood of Los Angeles, CA

PRODUCT MURAL

Hand-painted product **murals** are a common sight in parts of San Diego and East and Central Los Angeles, as they are across Latin America and especially in Mexico. The widespread tradition likely traveled north with Latino shopkeepers. Product murals depict anything from loaves of bread to dishwashing soap, showcasing a wide variety of goods. In fact, just about anything that can be sold may end up on a storefront facade.

Although the choice to use product murals is usually an economic one, this style of graphic communication has other practical purposes. Product pictures are a visual means to convey store merchandise to a diverse, multilingual clientele. Advertising with images also helps po-

tential clients decipher the subtle merchandising differences among small general markets that may carry a highly eclectic assortment of goods—from tortillas and toasters to batteries and lipstick.

For many, commercial murals offer aesthetic relief from an endless landscape of Helvetica signage and strip-mall homogeneity. For graphic designers in particular, Latino neighborhoods are a gold mine of inspiration for the lost art of hand lettering. Type designer Christian Schwartz (1977–) cites vernacular script as the inspiration for his Los Feliz font, named for the Hollywood-adjacent neighborhood where the signage was found. *See also Mural.*

Randy's Donuts (1953) offers up a selection of delectible donuts 24/7, but it's the one on top that has made this building a beloved landmark in Inglewood, CA

PROGRAMMATIC ARCHITECTURE

Programmatic architecture is a term to describe structures built to mimic the name or function of a business. To capture the attention of passing motorists, savvy owners have erected everything from tamales and **hot dogs** to toads and teapots, all of which have contributed to a cornucopia of roadside amusements. Most were designed as counter-service establishments where customers could buy chili out of a chili bowl or film from the lens of a camera. Among the genre's most famous was Los Angeles's hat-shaped Brown Derby restaurant (1926–1980), where the Cobb salad and the Shirley Temple cocktail were born. Southern California was once so well known for these architectural oddities that they were dubbed California Crazy style.

The vernacular movement prevailed as the region's car culture developed, from the 1920s to the 1950s. Two-story cowboy boots and the like dwindled in the 1950s as architects focused their talents away from novelty experience and toward eye-catching signage. Like the recent loss of Hollywood's iconic Tail o' the Pup hot dog stand, most programmatic establishments remain only as memories. However, patrons of Randy's Donuts in Inglewood and the Donut Hole in La Puente can experience their purchases at Brobdingnagian scale, and a Cadillac-shaped **strip mall** in Tarzana gives shoppers the impression of walking into the front end of a vintage Caddie. *See also Fantasy Architecture and Strip Mall.*

A Jimmy Choo employee awaits customers at the South Coast Plaza Mall in Costa Mesa, CA

SHOPPING MALL

Given that shopping malls were designed to introduce the consumer choices of a traditional downtown to the car-dependent suburbs, it is ironic that these structures were pioneered by a staunchly Socialist European émigré who hated cars and later disparaged his own invention. After his initial mall successes in the Midwest, Victor Gruen (1903–1980) set up shop in Southern California, where his prototype has flourished.

While still at the heart of modern consumer culture, shopping malls have gone through immense changes over the nearly six decades of their existence, mimicking the hormonal transformations of the teens they tend to attract. Having evolved from **strip malls** and pedestrian shopping corridors, mall developments were initially enclosed structures for food courts, department stores, and specialty boutiques. Newer styles, like the Grove in Los Angeles, resemble Disneyesque streetscapes—open-air, pedestrian-friendly lifestyle malls, with gurgling fountains, upscale retailers, and Zagat-rated restaurants. Also widespread are power centers—behemoth strip malls anchored by big-box retailers and surrounded by acres of parking.

Love them or hate them, shopping malls have had a deep impact on modern living—from the speech of teenagers to the lure of suburbia. As retail spending shifts online and leisure time dwindles, shopping malls will continually evolve as the town squares of the modern era. *See also Strip Mall.*

Josh Cadena captures a video of his friend and fellow skater, Mike Franklin, as they skateboard in Santa Clarita, CA • Jason Grillo

SKATEBOARDING

Surfers took to the activity of "sidewalk **surfing**" sometime in the 1940s or 1950s as a fun alternative when waves were flat. They skimmed "asphalt waves" using boards or wooden boxes with roller-skate wheels attached. The first patented skateboard, with clay wheels, appeared in 1958, but skating didn't attain mainstream appeal until the introduction of smoother-riding polyurethane wheels in 1972.

A new breed of skateboarding arrived in the summer of 1976, after a serious drought left many **swimming pools** empty. The Z-Boys of Dogtown (Z for the Santa Monica Zephyr surf shop, Dogtown for the neighborhood) would scout drained pools, bringing their own hoses and pumps to remove stagnant water. The exposed, curved walls allowed for a whole new style of vertical maneuvers and speed that made the skateboarders famous. While they originally started their skate team to improve their surfing, the Z-Boys—in particular, Tony Alva (1957–), Jay Adams (1961–2014), and Stacy Peralta (1957–)—swept competitions with their amazing feats, becoming a national skateboard sensation.

SoCal skate culture has a long reach, inspiring BMX, snowboarding, and other extreme sports, as well as Orange County–based companies such as Quiksilver, Rip Curl, Roxy, Ocean Pacific, and Vans—all of which have defined the classic skater look. *See also Surfing.*

A view of downtown Los Angeles from a vista in Runyon Canyon Park in Los Angeles, CA

SMOG

The term *smog*—a clever blending of the words *smoke* and *fog*—was coined at the turn of the 20th century to identify a type of air pollution synonymous with Los Angeles. As a basin settlement encircled by mountains with little yearly rainfall to wash the pollution away, the region has endured this noxious affliction for centuries. As early as 1542, the Portuguese-born Spanish explorer Juan Rodríguez Cabrillo (1499–1543) noted a layer of smoke from the Indian fires burning inland as he sailed into San Pedro Bay. He consequently named the waters the Bahía de Los Fumos (Smoke Bay).

Today a more dangerous type of smog is created from chemical reactions among the sun's ultraviolet radiation, nitrogen oxides (from the exhaust of cars, trucks, cargo ships, and manufacturing plants), and volatile organic compounds (released from gasoline, paints, pesticides, and solvents, as well as natural emissions). By the early 1940s Los Angeles's unfortunate geography and expanding car culture had engendered a smog problem that bore serious consequences for the health of the city's citizens, prompting Los Angeles County to launch the nation's first air pollution control agency in 1947. Although catalytic converters, cleaner gasoline, smog checks, and stricter industrial standards have helped Californians make enormous strides in reducing smog, air quality remains among of the most foul in the nation. *See also Freeway and Oil Pump.*

The Watsu Pool inside SpaTerre at the Palm Springs Riviera Resort & Spa in Palm Springs, CA • Courtesy of the Palm Springs Riviera Resort & Spa

SPA

Southern California is blessed with natural hot springs, but it is the region's obsession with **health**, beauty, and indulgence that informed the spa concept. Spas run the gamut from no-frills natural springs in the far-flung regions of the Mojave Desert to exclusive resorts. For some destinations, heated water is the only attraction; others offer a myriad of health and relaxation activities such as saunas, body treatments, yoga, catered menus, and spiritual guidance. "Taking the waters" is an established element of regional culture, and those who enjoy a warm soak won't have to travel far to find one.

Native Americans were the first inhabitants to enjoy the curative powers of hot water, notably the ancestors of the Agua Caliente Band of Cahuilla Indians. They named the Palm Springs area Sec-he (boiling water); the Spanish, in turn, named it Agua Caliente (hot water). In the late 1880s health seekers flocked to similar restorative pools in such places as Carlsbad, Santa Fe Springs, and Arrowhead Springs. Increasingly, hot water is just another option in a long list of rejuvenating therapies and procedures at spa facilities. Today's ethnic spas, especially the Korean and Russion varieties, offer a balance between the simplicity of heated waters and indulgent pampering. *See also Health and Fitness.*

The historic Casa del Herrero (1925) in Montecito, CA, designed by local resident George Washington Smith, one of the most accomplished architects of Spanish Colonial Revivalism

SPANISH COLONIAL REVIVAL STYLE

Southern California's pervasive stucco structures and red-tiled roofs, which originated in the state's early **mission** and rancho architecture, re-emerged in the late 1800s in a style called **Mission Revival**. But the lasting legacy of these forms is owed to Spanish Colonial Revivalism, first seen in the Spanish Baroque buildings designed by Bertram Goodhue (1869–1924) for the 1915 Panama–California Exposition held in San Diego's Balboa Park. Inspired by Spain's Moorish, Andalusian, and Churrigueresque architecture, Goodhue elevated Mission Revival from rustic mimicry to sophisticated adaptation. Decorative tile, woodwork, stucco, and wrought-iron details added charming flourishes to otherwise plain exteriors. In contrast to the unrestrained embellishments of the Victorian age, the careful balance of austerity and ornamentation fit well within the era's embrace of the Arts and Crafts movement.

Two factors contributed to the widespread use of the Spanish Colonial Revival style by the 1920s: the increased exposure of servicemen and touring architecture students to the quaint vernacular styles of Spain and Portugal during World War I and the ability to record these styles with the relatively new medium of photography.

Several municipalities in Southern California, including Santa Barbara, mandated the Spanish Colonial Revival style, which helped to establish a distinctive regional identity. *See also Mission and Mission Revival Style.*

Originally built on a film studio lot in Culver City, the Spadena House (1921) now resides in a residential neighborhood in Beverly Hills, CA

STORYBOOK STYLE

Inspired in part by the vernacular peasant dwellings of Europe, California's storybook homes convey an old-world charm that would lure modern-day Hansels and Gretels. These hobbit houses combine crooked windows, cobblestone chimneys, curved wooden doors, mock thatched roofs, and heavy, rolled eaves to create an intentional look of delightful dilapidation. Storybook style homes first came on the scene in the early 1920s and all but disappeared by the end of the Depression.

Hollywood, the ultimate land of make-believe, became the epicenter of storybook style, partially due to the city's propensity for fantasy and the unconventional, but also for the expert skills of movie-set designers who could realize residential fairy tales. The film industry not only helped to propagate the style, but was inspired by it as well. Many speculate that storybook homes provided inspiration for the cozy abode of the Seven Dwarves, from Disney's animated feature *Snow White* (1937).

Although somewhat rare, Storybook structures are easy to spot. Examples can be found scattered throughout Southern California in Los Angeles, Long **Beach**, Pasadena, Hollywood, and even Beverly Hills, where art director Harry Oliver's (1888–1973) 1921 masterpiece, known as the Spadena House, or Witch's House, now resides.

Field workers pick a fall strawberry harvest in Oxnard, CA

STRAWBERRY FIELD

Between Los Angeles and Santa Barbara lies California's Strawberry Coast, where acres of strawberry fields thrive in the area's cool and moist ocean breezes. Planted in elevated rows and mulched in plastic, strawberry plants cover nearly 15,000 acres across Southern California, with the center of growth in Oxnard, Ventura County. Farms from this locale harvest and ship more than 200,000 tons of berries each year, bringing in an annual revenue of $300 million. Berries are picked, sorted, and packed by hand in the field, largely by Latino migrant workers, especially indigenous Oaxacans. Strawberry picking is one of the most difficult and lowest-paid farm jobs, requiring workers to stoop for long hours and be exposed to harmful pesticides. During peak season, picking is done every three days.

The state's long coastline allows for fruit almost year-round, making strawberries a perpetual sight at farmers' markets. Harvest begins in fall and early winter and moves north throughout the season. In Oxnard, May is peak season, marked by the city's beloved Strawberry Festival. Here it is possible to eat the national yearly average of strawberries—eight pounds per person—in just a few hours, with offerings such as strawberry shortcake, strawberry kabobs, strawberry pizza, strawberry nachos, and even strawberry beer.

Shops are advertised high and large at a Harbor City, CA strip mall

STRIP MALL

The strip mall, a reviled cousin of the **shopping mall**, evolved out of rampant car culture and embodies the ultimate architecture of convenience. Although strip malls are not indigenous to the region, they have become a defining feature of the Southern California streetscape, in large part responsible for the inescapable suburban feel of the region. These famously bland structures are the refuge of convenience stores, check-cashing businesses, self-service laundries, nail salons, and doughnut shops—the last bastion of mom-and-pop establishments.

Linear commercial development first took root in the 1920s, and by the 1970s and 1980s, strip mall construction mushroomed, erasing any evidence of the gas stations that typically preceded them. (Gas station lots, commercially zoned on well-situated corners, became widely available following the 1973–74 **oil** crisis.)

For those who have embraced the strip mall, whether by choice or practicality, there are treasures to discover. In ethnic neighborhoods, strip malls have become centers of the local diaspora, selling exotic goods from faraway homelands such as South Korea, Armenia, Vietnam, and Iran. And although mini-malls are far from stylish, their cheap rents attract a surprising contingent of cutting-edge galleries, trendy restaurants, and designer boutiques. Let's face it, in SoCal, it's a mall world after all. *See also Shopping Mall.*

Lighting equipment and wardrobe racks on a soundstage at the Warner Brothers studio lot in Burbank, CA • Jordan Parhad

STUDIO LOT

America's earliest movies were shot on the East Coast in the early 1900s. Without patent rights to use film technology, independent producers were plagued by lawsuits, prompting them to venture west. Before long, Los Angeles was discovered to be a filmmaker's heaven, with a sunny climate, breathtaking landscapes, willing workers, and cheap rent.

The West's first commercial movie was made in Los Angeles in 1908, and the first studio—Nestor Film Company—opened in 1911. Rooftops, empty barns, and vacant lots (where the word *lot* originates) provided the ideal setups for filming, allowing bright sunshine to expose early film stock. By the 1930s the Big Five (Metro-Goldwyn-Mayer/ MGM, RKO Radio Pictures, 20th Century–Fox, Warner Bros., and Paramount), and the Little Two (Columbia and Universal) were movie factories, churning out "flickers" at incredible speed. Studios required long-term contracts with creative personnel, and they controlled every aspect of film production in-house, including financing, marketing, and distribution. Antitrust cases radically changed this old studio system, making today's studios more akin to huge service providers than the monopolistic behemoths they once were.

Several studios offer fascinating tours of their facilities, but only one— Paramount—remains in Hollywood proper. Most other lots are located in Culver City or the San Fernando Valley. *See also Celebrity, Film Location Sign, Movie Palace, and Pornography.*

Surfers revel in the waves at a beach in San Clemente, CA • David McShane

SURFING

Surfing originated in ancient Polynesian societies as a spiritual and pleasurable activity for the upper classes. In 1907 the railway magnate Henry Huntington (1850–1927) introduced surfing to California when he hired a Hawaiian native of Irish heritage named George Freeth (1883–1919) to showcase the joys of the sea in hopes of promoting his newly completed trolley service from Los Angeles to Redondo **Beach**. By today's standards, Freeth's board was enormous, weighing 200 pounds and measuring more than 10 feet long. Although the stunt was successful, a mass following didn't occur until the 1950s, when lighter boards became available.

The golden age of surfing coincided with a time when teenagers were becoming the tastemakers of pop culture. Teenage beach party films, such as Gidget, and pop music bands, such as the Beach Boys, helped to evangelize surfing, and the endless summers and leisurely living of Southern California. Long boards and wood-paneled station wagons, called woodies, became the icons of this enviable lifestyle.

Now surfing is a multibillion-dollar industry that still defines the informal beach culture of Southern California. While a much greater diversity of surfers and riding styles exists, the quest for the perfect wave remains a constant. *See also Skateboarding.*

Low rays of sunlight highlight early morning mist at the Renaissance Esmeralda Resort & Spa pool in Indian Wells, CA

SWIMMING POOL

Since the first private pool in Southern California was built in 1920 at Pickfair, the Beverly Hills estate of actors Douglas Fairbanks (1883–1939) and Mary Pickford (1892–1979), the pool has been an image of the region's fabled life of leisure, youth, and endless sunshine. As other movie stars followed suit, even those who could not swim, the backyard pool was destined to become the ultimate status symbol.

The middle class finally got in on the fun in the postwar era, when suburbia offered the space for pools, and working-class weekenders lounged poolside at Palm Springs–area motels. In the mid-1970s a severe drought forced the emptying of pools, revealing the perfect surface for **skateboarding**—a sport that would become a defining subculture of Southern California.

Intertwined into a diverse mix of California landscapes and identities, the swimming pool has long been a fascinating subject for artists. Photographers Craig R. Stecyk III (1951–) captured Dogtown skateboarders in waterless pools, Ed Ruscha (1937–) created a series of nine lonely waters, and Julius Shulman (1910–2009) showcased **midcentury modern** backyard oases. No artist more fully explored the theme than David Hockney (1937–), whose work includes Polaroid photo collages, poolside paintings, and renderings of Hollywood's Roosevelt Hotel pool, where he embellished the surface with blue squiggles that seem to swirl to life with moving waters.

Grilled halibut tacos at El Pescador Fish Market in La Jolla, CA

TACO

The taco is to Southern California what pizza is to New York. The specialty of **food trucks** and pop-up street vendors, tacos offer satisfaction with simple architecture—tortillas filled with meat and toppings with **salsa** on the side. The popularity of the taco is due in part to its versatility—tortillas can be corn or wheat, soft or fried, and the possibilities for fillings are endless: *carne asada* (grilled beef), *al pastor* (spit-grilled pork), *carnitas* (braised pork), *nopales* (cactus) and more.

Further south, near San Diego, the fish taco gains prominence. The Baja-style taco consists of deep-fried, battered white fish, such as cod, in a corn tortilla piled with shredded cabbage, *pico de gallo* (an uncooked salsa), lime, and a cream sauce.

The origin of the fish taco is ambiguous. Some say Japanese fishermen brought the tempura-style batter to Baja in the 1930s; others insist the taco appeared with the start of the Ensenada fish market in 1958. While surfers had been talking up this local specialty for years, Ralph Rubio (1956–) introduced the fish taco north of the border on a large scale in 1983 with his Rubio's chain.

Surprisingly, tacos showed up in California as late as the 1920s and only became widespread after the arrival of the Irvine-based Taco Bell franchise in the 1960s. *See also Chips and Salsa and Food Truck.*

Green chile and cheese tamales are prepared for steaming at a family tamalada party in Alhambra, CA

TAMALE

In this land of **fast-food** offerings, tamales are the culinary black sheep. These corn husk-wrapped packets of *masa* (corn-based dough), stuffed with a variety of fillings, often take an entire day to make. Family *tamaladas* (tamale-making parties) use the hands of many to tackle the tasks of preparing the filling, lathering masa on *hojas* (corn husks), folding them up, and steaming or boiling the finished package. The reward is eating the tamales together for special events—most importantly, Christmas dinner, where tamales are a well-known Latino tradition. Typical fillings include chile-braised pork, green chile and cheese, vegetables, stewed chicken, and, for those who like a sweeter tamale, fruits or seasonal green corn.

Tamales date to pre-Columbian times but arrived in Los Angeles sometime in the 1880s. *Tamaleros* hawked their goods out of horse-drawn wagons to a rough clientele in and around Olvera Street, the original site of Los Angeles pueblo. The Orange County-based food writer, Gustavo Arellano (1978–), writes that tamaleros offered up L.A.'s original street food and were "crucial ambassadors for the growth of Mexican food here—and in a region wedded to transit, their movable feasts laid the tracks for drive-thrus, lunch trucks and our insatiable fascination with easy-to-find, affordable grub."

In their day, tamales were as iconic to the city as Disneyland is to the region today. Though not the food **celebrity** they once were, tamales remain a beloved food, especially when made by friends and family.

Parkgoers enjoy the sights on Disneyland's "It's a Small World" boat ride in Anaheim, CA

THEME PARK

With more than a dozen theme parks, Southern California easily ranks as the theme park capital of the world. Even a century ago, the coasts were lined with seaside amusement parks situated on **piers**, much like the venerable Belmont Park in San Diego. Amusement parks segregated the rides, games, concessions, and sideshows into separate areas and, by the early 20th century, had garnered shady reputations. When Walt Disney (1901–1966) reimagined this setup by offering five themed areas and matching attractions in a clean, family-friendly environment, the industry changed forever. Disneyland opened in 1955, when themed environments were a decades-old fascination in Southern California, found in **cafeterias**, **tiki** lounges, shopping districts, and **storybook** homes.

Sparked by Disney's overwhelming success, similar parks opened across the state, and by the 1980s, theme parks were a multibillion-dollar industry. Through constant innovation, many historic parks have survived, including Knott's Berry Farm, which predates Disneyland by 15 years. Credited as America's first theme park, the farm re-created an entertaining gold rush boomtown for patrons waiting to try the farm's famous fried chicken.

From SeaWorld's marine animals to Universal **Studios**' movie magic, each park has its own strengths, history, and atmosphere, helping to entice millions of tourists to the region each year. *See also Fantasy Architecture and Pier.*

Tiki God and Hula Girl on the hood of "The Tiki Mobile," the Tiki-themed Jeep of "Tiki Al,"
a Tiki lifestyle devotee from Los Angeles, CA

TIKI CULTURE

When Hollywood's Don the Beachcomber restaurant opened in 1934, it inaugurated a trend of stylized head carvings, flower leis, flaming rum drinks, and rattan furniture. The fashionable setting was the result of a cleverly constructed mash-up of Polynesian cultures, soon emulated for a more upscale clientele at the Trader Vic's chain and numerous other eateries. After World War II, the appeal of Polynesian Pop peaked with the return of servicemen stationed in the South Seas, and then snowballed into the realms of music, literature, cuisine, theater, and architecture.

Stylistically, the Tiki theme was well suited to America's midcentury tastes, adapted to apartment complexes, motels, bowling alleys, and drive-ins as well as suburban rumpus rooms and yard parties. By the 1960s the movement was global, and nearly every neighborhood in Southern California boasted at least one garden of the gods. As Vietnam War veterans began to return home in the 1970s, however, an escape to the tropics became ill suited to the times. Most temples to Tiki gradually gave way to decay or corporate takeover, though some excellent examples of this quirky chapter of Americana remain, such as Tiki Ti's Bar in Silver Lake. Some say a major Tiki resurgence is looming, evidenced in part by the new Don the Beachcomber that opened in Huntington **Beach** in 2009. Mai tai, anyone? *See also Fantasy Architecture, Programmatic Architecture, and Theme Park.*

A valet attends his station at the classic 1950s Dal Rae Restaurant in Whittier, CA

VALET PARKING

Valet parking is as much a part of the restaurant and nightclub scene in Southern California as doggie bags and DJs. Despite its association with elitism, valet parking has become an expected amenity in the region, found everywhere from the trendiest eateries and country clubs to hospitals, airports, supermarkets, and **shopping malls**. In addition to reinforcing a car owner's self-importance, valet service provides vehicle security and convenience as well as decreasing incidents of drunken driving and minimizing traffic jams. For less money than most bars charge for a drink, a uniformed attendant will perform the arduous task of finding parking in a land famous for confusing parking signage and hard-to-find spots. For a little extra, he or she will retrieve items from a vehicle or have it washed and detailed. Finally, when the driver is ready—zip!—the car magically appears again.

Parking concessions have been around for about as long as cars, but the Lord of the Lot, Herb Citrin (1922–2013), turned the service into an industry. In 1946 Mr. Valet, as he was also known, started Valet Parking Service at Lawry's The Prime Rib in Beverly Hills, providing the term for the occupation. His decades of experience inspired the Herb Citrin Trophy, given to the world's best valet team at the National Valet Parking Association's Valet Olympics.

A mural of the Virgin of Guadalupe in the Boyle Heights neighborhood of Los Angeles, CA

VIRGIN OF GUADALUPE

As the patron saint of Mexico and a potent symbol of the Chicano movement across America, the Virgin of Guadalupe may be Southern California's most beloved icon. Huge crowds gather at shrines, feasts, and processions to honor her on her feast day, December 12. Her pervasive image—seen in **murals**, home altars, neighborhood grottos, sidewalk shrines, and even kitsch products—is a testament to the profound meaning she holds for so many.

Also called Our Lady of Guadalupe, she first appeared in Mexico in 1531 to Juan Diego, a Nahuatl (Aztec) convert to Christianity, to request that a church be built on the site. Her now familiar image, framed by rays of light and roses, references the miracle of the red blooms that accompanied her, despite the dark December day. Juan Diego placed the flowers in his *tilma* (poncho), where her likeness later appeared to a church official.

For believers, most of whom are Latino Catholics, the Virgin of Guadalupe is a fundamental symbol of their faith and an irrefutable reminder of the cultural roots that Southern California shares with Mexico. In 2011, when an anonymous mural in Encinitas appeared depicting the Virgin as a surfer, it affirmed what many already know—Our Lady of Guadalupe may not be a native, but she most certainly is a local. *See also Botanica.*

Leonard Knight used over 100,000 gallons of paint over hay and dirt to create Salvation Mountain in Niland, CA

VISIONARY ENVIRONMENT

Visionary environments are permanent, large-scale installations made by self-taught artists who are dedicated to, and sometimes obsessed by, creating something fantastic. *Watts Towers* is the most well known of these awe-inspiring lifeworks, constructed over a 33-year period by an Italian immigrant named Simon Rodia (1875–1965). He "had in mind to do something big" and did so by applying bits of **decorative tile**, bottles, and other refuse onto steel rebar that reaches heavenward—a work Mr. Rodia himself called *Nuestra Pueblo* (Our Town).

Current works are always in the making, such as the sculpture gardens behind Tio's **Tacos** restaurant in Riverside; *Elmer's Bottle Tree Ranch* in Oro Grande; the *East Jesus Sculpture Garden* in Niland; and *Phonehenge West*, a complex fabricated with telephone poles in Acton, demolished in 2011. Not only can each of these pieces' existence be challenged by neighbors and building codes, but over time, these monuments pose difficulties to preservation after the artist is gone. The Noah Purifoy Outdoor Desert Art Museum in Joshua Tree, *Bottle Village* by Grandma Prisby (1896–1988) in Simi Valley, and *Old Trapper Lodge* by John Ehn (1897–1981), moved to the grounds of Pierce College in Woodland Hills from Burbank, have all been affected by **earthquakes**, weather, and time. Their inspiration lives on as amazing environments for visitors to explore, not only in the physical sense, but for the insight they bring to the workings of an artist's mind.

Water gushes down falls at the Cascades section of the Los Angeles Aqueduct in Sylmar, CA

WATER WAR

Thanks to imported water, Southern California's fertile valleys and tropical landscaping give the impression of a lush paradise. In its natural state, however, the land is a semi-desert, at best. In Los Angeles especially, water has been a concern since the **mission** days, and by the turn of the 20th century, population needs outgrew supply. In 1908 construction began on what would become the longest aqueduct in the world, bringing water to the city from the Owens River in east-central California. William Mulholland (1855–1935) masterminded this ambitious project, spanning 233 mountainous miles and using only gravity to move water. This feat, considered to be one of the greatest engineering wonders of the modern era, was not without controversy. The secrecy with which Owens River Valley land rights were obtained and the $100 million worth of land speculation in the San Fernando Valley sparked the 25-year-long Owens Valley Water War and later inspired Roman Polanski's film *Chinatown* (1974).

With a 175-gallon-per-capita daily usage rate, water remains one of the most important issues facing the region. It's no wonder that the head of the Los Angeles Department of Water and Power is paid more than the mayor—a long-standing policy that is sure to continue far into the future.

A snowy egret at Bolsa Chica Ecological Reserve in Huntington Beach, CA • Jane E. Lazarz

WETLAND

Wetlands are shallow, low-lying areas where freshwater creeks and inland climates converge with the sea and coastal fogs. Tidal forces carry a constant ebb and flow of saltwater into a variety of fragile and unique environments—freshwater marsh, salt marsh, coastal sage scrub, and riparian woodland—that harbor an equally diverse mix of fish, invertebrates, mammals, and waterfowl. These areas help to purify outgoing water and minimize flooding and erosion. Wetlands also provide protective breeding grounds for fish and resting stops for migratory birds.

While California has more wetlands than any other state, it has also suffered the greatest losses—more than 90 percent of its wetland habitat—mostly to urbanization. Coastal areas have been dredged and filled to make way for airports, industrial complexes, housing developments, and marinas. The few wetlands that remain are far from pristine, but conservation efforts are under way to minimize damage in many areas.

Forty-one coastal wetland areas lie between Point Conception in Santa Barbara County and the Mexican border, and the majority of them are publicly owned. The most accessible of these are the salt marshes and lagoons between Long **Beach** and San Diego, where visitors can watch migrating birds, kayak, canoe, and hike. Favorites include the Bolsa Chica Ecological Reserve, as well as the San Elijo, Batiquitos, San Dieguito, and Los Peñasquitos Lagoons. *See also Beach.*

The 2009 Station Fire looms over a hilltop house in La Cañada Flintridge, CA

WILDFIRE

Southern California is a volatile fire environment that has no match in North America. Each year the California Department of Forestry and Fire Protection (Cal Fire) responds to an average of 6,300 fires across the state that destroy nearly 144,000 acres, not including fires fought by municipal crews. Fire season arrives in early summer—along with the hot, fire-fanning winds called the Santa Anas—and usually wanes with the rains of winter.

Millions of Californians live on the edge of fire country—namely **chaparral** scrublands, Southern California's most common vegetation. In the last decade alone, these residents have seen some of the largest and deadliest wildfires in California history. In 2003 fourteen simultaneous fires took 24 lives and burned 748,000 acres and 4,461 structures. Just four years later, more than a half-million people evacuated from their homes, from Ventura to Baja, when 23 major fires raged for more than a week across 517,000 acres.

Although hazardous for humans, wildfires are an important and endemic part of the state's ecology. Many plant species depend on this ancient cycle of destruction and rebirth for germination to occur. Lupines, phacelias, and **California poppies** are all pyrophytes, or fire followers, that thrive in postfire conditions. Their blooms transform charred landscapes into magnificent displays of color in the years after a fire, and then lie dormant until the next blaze occurs. *See also Chaparral.*

HISTORY, INDUSTRY, AND INFLUENCES

• 20,000–15,000 BC •

Ancestors of California's native peoples migrate across the Bering Strait and into California from northeast Asia.

• 1500s •

Portuguese-born explorer, Juan Rodríguez Cabrillo (1499-1543), arrives at present-day San Diego and claims California for Spain in 1542.

• 1700s •

California's first **MISSION**, San Diego de Alcalá, is established in 1769. By 1823 Spanish missionaries had founded 21 missions and numerous villages between San Diego and Sonoma.

El Pueblo de la Reyna de los Angeles (one of several disputed original names), now known as the City of Los Angeles, is founded in 1781.

• 1800s •

Mexico gains **INDEPENDENCE** from Spain in 1821. California becomes a U.S. Territory in 1848 and is admitted into the Union as the 31st state two years later.

Mexico secularizes the missions and distributes enormous **LAND GRANTS** to well-connected families, giving rise to the state's **CATTLE RANCHING** industry.

The completion of the **TRANSCONTINENTAL RAILROAD** in 1869 attracts droves of **TOURISTS**, **ADVENTURERS**, **LABORERS**, and enterprising **BUSINESSMEN** to California, vastly increasing its pace of urbanization, industrialization, and agricultural development.

• 1800s, Cont. •

At the close of the 19th century, **BOOSTERS** heavily advertise Southern California's eternal sunshine, thriving **CITRUS INDUSTRY,** and pastoral romance of the old mission days. The state's population explodes from 380,000 in 1860 to almost 3.5 million in 1920.

• 1900s •

Production companies head to Hollywood for **MOVIEMAKING** in the early 1900s to make use of the climate and avoid legal patent issues back East.

The Los Angeles **AQUEDUCT** is completed in 1913, allowing for the massive future development of the region.

The rise of the **AUTOMOBILE** in the 1920s mobilizes the populace and gears urbanization towards individualized, four-wheeled travel.

The **OIL, AGRICULTURE**, and **ENTERTAINMENT** industries of the 1920s and 1930s attract millions of people to Southern California, helping the region overtake Northern California as the economic engine of the state.

AEROSPACE and **SHIPPING** industries emerge during World War II, bringing millions of more workers to California. Further migration increases postwar, fueling a boom in **HIGHWAY** and **HOUSING CONSTRUCTION, SUBURBANIZATION**, and the **MODERNIZATION** of the home.

• 2000s •

By the first decade of the 21st century, California is the world's 12th largest economy with a population of 24 million.

CONTRIBUTORS

Catherine Comeau
COPY EDITOR
inkprojects.com

Susanne Duffner
DESIGNER & COVER
PHOTOGRAPHER
susanneduffnerdesign.com

Danielle Roderick
WRITER
Twitter: @droderi

Ning Tay
WRITER

Alexander Vidal
PHOTOGRAPHER
inkandtonic.com

Jordan Parhad
PHOTOGRAPHER

Paul Richter
PHOTOGRAPHER

Jason Grillo
PHOTOGRAPHER
OneEighteen Photography

Asia Pacific Offset
PRINTER
asiapacificoffset.com

ABOUT THE AUTHOR

Elisa Parhad
AUTHOR & PHOTOGRAPHER
Photo by Marsais Parhad

A cultural anthropologist at heart and by trade, Elisa Parhad is passionate about exploring place, space, design, and culture. After completing Bachelors degrees in Cultural Anthropology and International Business at the University of Texas at Austin, she spent many years studying American subcultures and communities to inform marketing messaging and advertising campaigns. Elisa lives in Pasadena with her husband and two sons.

To submit comments, suggestions, photographs,
or to just say hello, please write to
hello@eyemusebooks.com.

To order this and other *Guides for the Eyes* books
visit www.eyemusebooks.com.